"Wow—if you're looking for a fresh devotional on the Gospel of Mark which packages the best scholarship into 100 bite-sized portions that your pre-teens will love to read, then look no further. This is the best study of Mark for this age group that I've ever seen. Older children (and their parents!) will find each 2-page devotional engaging (Chris is a brilliant storyteller), enlightening (he's a master teacher), and incredibly encouraging (again and again he shines the spotlight on our Savior)! I hope you'll get copies for the pre-teens and young people in your life—and then read it with them!"

Champ Thornton, Pastor; Author, *The Radical Book for Kids*; Host, *In the Word, On the Go* podcast for families.

"What a brilliantly accessible, highly engaging Bible reading resource *Best News Ever* is for both tweens and their families. The daily descriptive commentary on a short passage is chatty, readable and clear, and packed with helpful explanations and relevant illustrations. A great easy-to-use tool to help young people see Jesus' character in the richness of Mark's Gospel."

Tamar Pollard, Youth and Children's Worker, Grace Community Church, Bedford, UK; Author, *Epic Explorers*

"*Best News Ever* walks us through Mark's Gospel to see and learn and think through how the truth about Jesus might change our lives forever. It's a great mix of detail, background and big picture, delivered in really manageable, day-by-day readings."

Colin Buchanan, Singer/songwriter

"*Best News Ever* is an excellent tool for parents and pastors to place in the hands of their maturing child. For those who are passionate about passing the faith on to the next generation, this is a vital tool for the young Christian seeking to deepen their understanding of the gospel of Jesus Christ."

Dr. John Perritt, Director of Resources, Reformed Youth Ministries (rym.org); Author, *Mark: How Jesus Changes Everything, Insecure,* and *Time Out!*

"*Best News Ever* makes a way for my ten-year-old to independently spend 100 days reading, learning, and praying through the Gospel of Mark. Morphew warmly invites pre-teen readers to engage with the Biblical text first and then acts as a friendly tutor, guiding them through context, comprehension, application, and prayer. As a mother of five, I'm grateful to find a hands-on tool to assist growing disciples as they learn to walk confidently and responsibly through Scripture."

Lindsey Carlson, Author, *Growing in Godliness: A Teen Girl's Guide to Maturing in Christ*

"Chris Morphew moves through the life of Jesus with the creativity of a novelist, the clarity of an experienced teacher, and the passion of someone deeply devoted to Jesus Christ. By letting Mark's Gospel tell the gospel, *Best News Ever* makes good on the promise of its title. I highly recommend it!"

John Dickson, Historian and Author, *Is Jesus History?* and *Hanging In There*

"Are you looking for a great way to engage your kids in God's word? Chris Morphew's devotional connects older children and young people with the Gospel of Mark to discover Jesus—the only one who can give us lasting joy. Truly the Best News Ever!"

Barbara Reaoch, Author, *A Jesus Christmas*

"*Best News Ever* is a practical, accessible and contemporary guide through the Gospel of Mark. It's the perfect growth tool for middle graders considering Christ."

Tim Harris, Author, *Exploding Endings* and *Mr Bambuckle's Remarkables* series

"*Best News Ever* is beautifully written, such that the reader is turning the page always eager for more. Chris Morphew is able to faithfully explain profound theology with simplicity and clarity. Highly recommended!"

Stuart Coulton, Principal, Sydney Missionary and Bible College

"Reading Chris Morphew's *Best News Ever* is like having a friendly conversation with him about the Gospel of Mark. I recommend every pre-teen and young person to have this book by their bedside."

Dr Paul Burgis, Executive Principal, Presbyterian Ladies' College, Sydney

CHRIS MORPHEW

BEST NEWS EVER

YOUR 100-DAY GUIDE TO THE GOSPEL OF MARK

thegoodbook
COMPANY

Best News Ever
© Chris Morphew 2019. Reprinted 2021.

Published by:
The Good Book Company

thegoodbook.com | thegoodbook.co.uk
thegoodbook.com.au | thegoodbook.co.nz | thegoodbook.co.in

ISBN: 9781784984373 | Printed in the UK

Design by André Parker

⚏ Contents ⚏

Introduction

Two thousand years ago, in an out-of-the-way corner of the Roman Empire, a dead man got up and walked out of his grave, and the world was changed forever.

By dying and coming back to life, this man not only proved that he was the King that God had promised would rule his people forever—he also made a way for anyone anywhere to follow him through death and out the other side, into never-ending life with God. These are the mind-blowing claims that Mark makes in his biography of Jesus—claims that have transformed the lives of billions of people around the world.

Maybe these ideas are brand new to you. Maybe you've heard them all before, but you wonder whether you can actually believe them. Maybe other people have been telling you about Jesus your whole life, but now you want to figure him out for yourself. Or maybe you're already following Jesus, and you want to get to know him better.

Whatever the case, I've designed this book to help you investigate Jesus for yourself, by guiding you through the whole of Mark's Gospel in a hundred short daily readings.

Each day, I'll invite you to do four things...

1. Read the next bit of Mark in the Bible

I've written *Best News Ever* to be like a window— something you look through to see the bigger, better, way-more-interesting thing on the other side.

Reading this book without also reading Mark's Gospel is kind of like looking at a window just to admire the glass, and ignoring the spectacular sunrise outside. So whatever you do, don't skip this step!

If you don't already have a Bible, you can probably pick one up wherever you got this book, or else you can read the whole thing online for free (at www.biblegateway.com).

There are a bunch of different English translations of the Bible out there (because a bunch of different experts have translated the Bible from its original languages into English). I used the New International Version (NIV) to write this book, so grab one of those if you can, but you should get on fine with any translation you pick.

2. Read the next bit of Best News Ever

Even after it's been translated into English, Mark's Gospel is still a two-thousand-year-old book written by someone living in a completely different culture to ours—

so it probably shouldn't surprise you if some of it is a bit confusing when you first read it.

Each day, I've written some notes to explain parts that might be unclear, catch you up on any historical/background information you might need to know, and show how the events of Mark's Gospel fit into the big picture of the whole Bible.

I definitely haven't answered every possible question—but hopefully, at the end of these hundred days, you'll come away with a pretty clear picture of what Mark's Gospel is all about.

3. Ask yourself a question

Part of what Mark wants to show us is that Jesus isn't *just* an interesting person from history. He's the God of the universe, who we can actually get to know personally and who wants to change our lives, here and now, today. And so, along with each day's reading, I've written a question designed to help you consider your own response to what you've read, and how you might apply what you're learning to your everyday life.

4. Pray

At the end of each day, I've also included a short prayer that you might like to pray as a way of talking to God about what you've been reading and thinking about.

Don't let my words limit you—you can talk to God about anything, anytime, anywhere, and know that he's listening and that he cares. But if you're someone who finds prayer a bit weird or confusing, or you just don't know what to say, hopefully my suggested prayers will give you a starting point.

And that's it! I really hope you enjoy this book and find it useful. If you stick with it, I honestly believe that the next hundred days could change your life—not because you've read *my* book, but because you've read Mark's book, and because you've seen that the good news of Jesus really is the best news ever!

CHRIS

★ ⬛ DAY 1 ⬛ ★
EUANGELION!
READ MARK I v I

When was the last time you heard a piece of really incredible news? News so huge and awesome and amazing that you were just *bursting* to share it?

Mark's first readers lived under the rule of the great and powerful Roman Empire. Whenever a new Roman emperor was crowned or when the Romans won a victory over their enemies, a message would go out across the empire: *Euangelion!*

Euangelion means "Good news!"

And not just any good news—huge, awesome, amazing, *life-changing* news!

Mark uses this word to begin his biography of Jesus. Right up front, he wants us to know that the message of Jesus is literally the best news ever!

When you think about your relationship with God, what comes to mind?

For many people, it's a whole bunch of rules and advice you should follow if you want to get God to like you.

But here Mark tells us that the message of Jesus is something completely different.

It's not good *advice*. It's good *news*!

The message of Jesus isn't a list of things you need to do to earn God's love.

It's a life-changing announcement of what Jesus has already done for you!

Out of the four biographies of Jesus in the Bible, Mark's is the most fast-paced and action-packed. The whole time, it's like Mark can't write fast enough to get down everything he wants to say—like the good news is bursting out of him:

"Jesus has come! And nothing will ever be the same."

Has anyone ever shared the message of Jesus with you before? Did they make it sound more like good advice or good news?

PRAYER

Lord God, thank you that the good news of Jesus has been so carefully recorded for us in the Bible. As I read Mark's biography of Jesus, please help me see what Mark was so excited about! Help me see how this *euangelion* is good news for me too! Amen.

⚑ DAY 2 ⚑

THE WAIT IS (ALMOST) OVER!

READ MARK 1 v 1-5

What's the longest you've ever waited for someone to keep a promise they made you? Did you sometimes start to wonder if they'd ever keep their promise at all?

God's people had been waiting *hundreds of years* for God to send the Messiah—the great King he'd promised would rule and bless his people, and free them from their enemies forever.

It had been a long, *long* wait.

But all through their history, through special messengers called prophets, God had dropped hints about what this Messiah would be like.

Here, Mark gives us a couple of quotes from the prophets Malachi and Isaiah, who lived hundreds of years before Jesus: *Right before the Messiah appears, God will send one last messenger to get everyone ready—to go out into the wilderness and announce his arrival* (v 2-3).

And then Mark drops the bombshell: *The last messenger has come. And his name is John the Baptist* (v 4).

John appears in the wilderness. He tells the people to *get ready*, because God is about to do something huge.

The people flock to John to be baptised—to be plunged into the river as an outward symbol of an inward choice: they're on board with John's message. They want to turn back to God and be ready for the Messiah's arrival.

The people are waiting. But they won't have to wait much longer. As always, God will keep his promises to his people.

After all these years, the Messiah is just around the corner.

Can you think of any promises that God has made to you in the Bible? How easy is it for you to believe that God will keep them? Why?

PRAYER

God, thank you for always keeping your promises—even if you don't always keep them as quickly as I might like. When it feels like you're taking *forever* to answer my prayers, please remind me of your faithfulness. Help me trust in your promises *and* in your perfect timing. Amen.

⚔ DAY 3 ⚔ ✶

CENTRE STAGE

✶ READ MARK 1 v 4-8 ✶

So John arrives to prepare the way for the Messiah, and (despite his interesting food and fashion choices, v 6) the crowds keep swarming out to meet him.

Some people even start wondering if John himself might be the Messiah. Maybe he's the one to defeat their Roman rulers and set God's people free!

And even though John's not the Messiah, it sure would be easy for him to fake it. He's got the fame. He's got the followers. It would be so easy for him to just grab all that power for himself.

But John doesn't buy into it.

You think I'm impressive? he says. *Just wait! When the true Messiah comes, I won't even be worthy to untie his shoelaces for him* (v 7).

John knows he isn't here to take centre stage.

He's here to shine his spotlight on the *real* star.

And as we keep reading, we'll see how all of us are invited to make this same choice.

As a fish is made for water, we are made to be with God—to be loved with his perfect love and to love him back. When we push God aside and try to live without him, we're pushing aside the abundant life we were created for.

And so God calls us to make the same decision that John made: to let Jesus take the starring role in our lives. Not because Jesus needs us, but because he knows we need him—and because it's the way we step into the true life and freedom that Jesus came to bring us.

Is letting Jesus take the starring role in your life a new idea for you? What do you think it would look like?

PRAYER

Loving God, thank you for inviting me into abundant life with you. When I'm tempted to push you aside and shine the spotlight on myself, please remind me of your incredible love for me, and show me what it means to let Jesus take centre stage in my life. Amen.

✌ DAY 4 ✊

A NEW BEGINNING

★ **READ MARK 1 v 9-11**

To the ancient world, the raging sea was a scary place. It was wild and uncontrollable, and it sank ships and drowned their crews—and so people came to use "the deep" and "the waters" as ways to describe all kinds of darkness and chaos.

Take the first words of the Bible: "In the beginning God created the heavens and the earth. Now the earth was formless and empty, darkness was over the face of the deep, and the Spirit of God was hovering over the waters. And God said, 'Let there be light,' and there was light" (Genesis 1 v 1-3).

The Bible opens with this amazing poetic image of God's Spirit soaring over the dark, empty nothingness before creation. And then... God speaks into the darkness.

His word creates a big, beautiful world—God's perfect kingdom! The perfect home for his children!

But that's not the world we live in now, is it?

Fast-forward to John, waist-deep in the river. Things have gone wrong in God's good world. It's still beautiful, but it's broken too.

But now here comes Jesus, this ordinary-looking man, down into the water to be baptised—and it's like the creation story all over again.

Again, God's Spirit hovers over the waters. Again, God's voice speaks words of life: "You are my Son, whom I love; with you I am well pleased" (Mark 1 v 11).

The world can feel like a very dark place sometimes. But God won't let it stay that way forever. In Jesus, a new creation has begun—and one day he will finish it. Through his own Son, God is rewriting the story.

Does the world ever seem like a dark, chaotic place to you? When? What difference might it make to trust that God has a plan to make all the wrong things right?

PRAYER

Lord, the world feels so filled with darkness sometimes. When I feel anxious or scared, please remind me that you haven't given up on us. Help me to remember that you've sent your own Son to mend your broken world and bring your children home to you. Amen.

★ ⚡ DAY 5 ⚡ ★

A NEW HERO

★ READ MARK 1 v 12-13

★

If yesterday's reading was a rewrite of creation, today's reading is a rewrite of the *second* major event in the Bible—only this time, there's a massive twist.

The creation account ends with God breathing life into the first human beings.

Then along came an enemy of God, who spun a lie to convince the first people to turn away from their Creator: *Your heavenly Father doesn't really love you. He's holding out on you! You won't truly be happy until you take control for yourself!*

The first people believed the lie. They ignored God and decided to do things their own way instead. They broke their perfect friendship with God—and everything else started breaking down too. God said that death and darkness would enter his perfect creation. God's people cut themselves off from God's kingdom.

But even back then, there was the whisper of a promise: a great hero was coming who would crush God's enemy and bring God's children home.

Fast-forward again, and here's Jesus being tempted by the *same* enemy who came to God's first people, in the very beginning.

Mark doesn't give us much detail here, but from the other biographies of Jesus in the Bible, we know that Satan tempts Jesus with the same basic lie he tried on God's first people: *You won't truly be happy until you take control for yourself!*

Only this time, it doesn't work.

Jesus rejects the lies of God's enemy. He proves that he's a *new* kind of human being—one who will always trust and obey his heavenly Father.

Here in the wilderness, Jesus proves that he's the hero his people have been waiting for.

How easy do you find it to truly believe that God loves you and wants what's best for you? Why is that?

PRAYER

God, so often I believe the same lies your first people did. So often, I do things my own way instead of trusting you. Thank you that Jesus came to live the perfect life I couldn't live, to make a way for me to come back home to you. Amen.

⊠ DAY 6 ⊠

TURN THE CAR AROUND

READ MARK 1 v 14-15

Imagine you're in the car, in an unfamiliar part of town, and whoever's driving doesn't really know where they're going. They turn a corner, and suddenly you realise several things at once.

First, this street is really narrow. Second, the cars parked along both sides are all facing your direction. Third, there's another car driving straight towards you.

What's going on here? You're going the wrong way down a one-way street!

So what's the solution? Well, you're partway there already: you've *realised* you're going the wrong way. But realising is only step one. Step two is making a u-turn. It's turning the car around!

In today's reading, Jesus has returned from the wilderness, and he's travelling through Galilee, proclaiming *good news*: "The kingdom of God has come near" (v 15).

To be in the kingdom of God means to enjoy living under God's good rule, with him as your King. So this "kingdom of God" is the *same* perfect kingdom that God's first people lived under way back in the beginning—before they tragically cut themselves off.

And the Bible says we've cut ourselves off from that kingdom too, by believing the same lie those first people did: that God doesn't really love us and that we'd be better off without him. And so we ignore God, reject him as King and decide to do things our own way instead. We cut ourselves off from God and his kingdom.

But now here's Jesus saying that the kingdom has come near again! He calls us, in response, to "repent" and "believe".

"Repenting" is making a u-turn. It's realising that we're going the wrong way, that we've been running from God.

But realising is only step one. Step two is turning the car around.

Jesus has come to be the great rescuer that God promised. He invites us to stop running from God and run to him instead.

When are you tempted to think that your way is better than God's way? What would it look like to "turn the car around"?

PRAYER

God, thank you that you sent Jesus to be my rescuer—so now there's nothing left for me to do but believe the good news and run back home to you. Amen.

⚌ DAY 7 ⚌
COME, FOLLOW ME
READ MARK 1 v 16-20

As Jesus travels around announcing the good news of God's kingdom, he finds four fishermen working on the shore of Lake Galilee. He invites them to leave everything and follow him.

And just like that, they do it.

These guys will spend the next *three years* following Jesus everywhere he goes.

Which raises a question: why on earth would they leave everything behind to follow a man they'd just met?

And the answer is... they didn't.

Mark does kind of make it look that way, but if we jump over to John's Gospel (John 1 v 35 – 2 v 12), we'll learn that this isn't actually the first time these guys have met.

These fishermen were once disciples of John the Baptist. They saw John announce that Jesus was the Messiah, and so they went and investigated Jesus for themselves.

They spent a bunch of time getting to know Jesus and were even there when he first displayed his way-more-than-human power by turning a few hundred litres of water into wine at a wedding.

So when Jesus arrives at the lake and invites these guys to follow him, they still don't know everything—not even close—but they've seen enough to know that Jesus is well worth following.

And so that's exactly what they do.

And through his Gospel, Mark is inviting you to do the same thing: to investigate Jesus for yourself and to find out what he's really like, so that you can come and follow him too.

How well do you think you know Jesus? Have you seen enough to decide that he's someone worth following?

PRAYER

Loving Father, as I keep reading through Mark's Gospel, please help me to see more and more of what Jesus is like—not just so that I can know more information about him, but so that I can get to know him as a real person who I can trust and follow. Amen.

⚔ DAY 8 ⚔

DRIVING OUT THE DARKNESS

READ MARK 1 v 21-28

So Jesus and his newly-recruited disciples come to Capernaum (a town on the edge of the Sea of Galilee that will be the closest thing Jesus has to a home base for the next few years).

It's the Sabbath—a Saturday—so they head for the synagogue, where God's people meet each week to study the Scriptures.

Jesus starts teaching the crowd gathered there. And already, they're super impressed, because it seems like Jesus isn't just repeating the same old messages of their other teachers (v 22). Something about the way Jesus talks about God's kingdom makes it sound like the words are coming straight from God himself!

But then suddenly, the meeting takes a dramatic turn.

There's a shout from across the room: the voice of a man who's been overtaken by the dark side. He's being controlled by a spirit who works for the same enemy of God that Jesus encountered, back out in the wilderness.

But remember, out there in the wilderness, Jesus has already proved that he can *resist* the powers of darkness.

And now he's going to show his power and authority to *drive out* those powers of darkness altogether—because those dark powers have no place in God's kingdom.

Jesus banishes the spirit, setting the man free from its control. And, understandably, the crowd is blown away.

Because here in the synagogue, we see another huge clue that Jesus hasn't just come to talk about God's kingdom.

He's here to bring that kingdom to Earth.

And he's here with the power to drive out the darkness, wherever he finds it.

How do you feel about the idea that these kinds of spiritual forces exist in our world? What difference does it make that Jesus has authority over these forces?

PRAYER

Loving Father, thank you for this amazing glimpse of Jesus' authority over the dark and broken things in this world. When I'm tempted to feel afraid or anxious about the scary things in my own life, remind me that the love of Jesus is greater than any power of darkness. Amen.

⊠ DAY 9 ⊠

POWER TO HEAL

★ READ MARK 1 v 29-34

★

After leaving the synagogue in Capernaum, Jesus and his disciples head down the road to Simon and Andrew's house, where Simon's mother-in-law (his wife's mother) is sick in bed.

Jesus helps her up...

And just like that, she's completely healed.

Now, if you already know a bit about Jesus, the idea that he could heal people might not be news to you. But it's *definitely* news to these guys.

This is the first time they've ever seen Jesus do something like this. And it brings them back to the question that the first half of Mark's Gospel is all about: who *is* Jesus?

How can he *do* all this?

And as we try to get to the bottom of this, something to keep an eye on is not just that Jesus *can do* impossible things, but *which* impossible things Jesus decides to do.

Jesus doesn't fly through the air here. He doesn't shoot lasers out of his eyes. He heals a sick woman of her fever.

Jesus' miracles are all about giving us a glimpse of who he is and what this kingdom he keeps announcing is all about.

Jesus *is* showing his power. But he's showing his power to make a point: *sickness and suffering have no place in the kingdom of God.*

And as we move through Mark's Gospel, we'll see that Jesus' individual healings are just the first flickering glimpses of a future where *all* sickness will be wiped out, once and for all, and God's kingdom will be fully revealed.

What does it tell us about Jesus that he would choose to use his power to help others like this?

PRAYER

Loving Father, when I feel frustrated and heartbroken by sickness, please remind me that you hate sickness just as much as I do—and that, in Jesus, you have a plan to one day get rid of that sickness and suffering once and for all. Amen.

⚡DAY 10⚡

WHO ARE YOU LISTENING TO?

READ MARK 1 v 35-39

Whose opinion matters most to you in the whole world? Who do you listen to when you've got an important decision to make?

For Jesus, the answer was clear: God his Father. He knew God loved him. He knew God could be trusted. Whatever anybody else said, it was his heavenly Father's opinion that mattered most to Jesus.

And so, the morning after everyone realises he has the power to heal, Jesus gets up before dawn to find a quiet place to pray.

Meanwhile, back at the house, a crowd is growing. The word about Jesus has kept spreading all night, and now more and more people are coming to see him and be healed.

Finally, the disciples track Jesus down, probably excited that he's so popular. They tell Jesus what's going on, and he says...

"Let us go somewhere else."

Wait. What?

All those sick people waiting to be healed, and Jesus wants to just get up and *leave*?

What's going on here?

Well, it's not that Jesus has given up healing people. And it's not that he doesn't care. But right now, Jesus has something *even more important* to do. He needs to keep preaching his good news about God's kingdom.

We'll find out exactly *why* that's more important soon.

In the meantime, another question: if Jesus himself regularly took the time to go somewhere quiet and pray, how much more important must that be for us?

When might be a regular time in your day that you could talk to your heavenly Father? What might you talk to him about?

PRAYER

God, there are so many voices that want to tell me how to live, but Jesus knew it was your opinion that mattered most. He knew that you loved him, and that he could trust you. Please help me to know that too, and to talk to you about all the things I care about. Amen.

⚌ DAY 11 ⚌

SWAPPING PLACES

READ MARK 1 v 40-45

As Jesus moves from village to village, he meets a man with leprosy, a contagious skin disease.

According to the law, anyone with leprosy was "unclean". They had to leave home, tear their clothes, grow out their hair and live outside in the lonely places. And if anyone came near, they had to cover their mouth and yell, "Unclean! Unclean!" to warn them off (Leviticus 13 v 45-46).

So this guy isn't just sick. He's banished from his home, his family—his whole life!

He's *desperate*.

So desperate that he breaks the don't-come-up-to-other-people law and crashes at Jesus' feet, begging to be made clean. In response, Jesus does something that no one has done to this guy in ages.

He reaches out and touches him.

Instantly, the man is healed. Even better, he can go *home!*

Jesus warns him not to tell anyone what's happened, but he's so overjoyed that he breaks that rule too! And as a result, the crowds wanting to see Jesus get so huge that he can't even go into a town without getting mobbed.

It's almost like Jesus has swapped places with the other man. He's been driven out to the lonely places so the other man can be welcomed home.

And here, we catch a glimpse of where this whole story is heading:

Jesus has come to make a way for God's people to come home to God—but it's going to cost him. To bring his people home, Jesus is going to have to take their place.

Can you think of a time when helping someone else has cost you something? What does it tell us about Jesus that he was willing to help this man, even though it meant swapping places?

PRAYER

Lord, it's amazing to see how Jesus not only healed this man's body but also made a way for him to go home again, even though it meant taking his place. As I keep reading through Mark, please help me see how Jesus came to swap places with me too. Amen.

⧑ DAY 12 ⧑

TRULY, FOREVER HAPPY

READ MARK 2 v 1-5

What do you look at and think, "If I could just have that, *then* I'd be happy!"?

A new phone? Some great achievement? A bit more money or popularity?

When Jesus gets home to Capernaum, he meets a man who's *sure* he knows what he needs to be happy. And he's so desperate to get it that he has his friends smash through a roof to put him in front of Jesus.

If he can just get his legs healed, *then* he'll be happy.

But Jesus has other plans: "Son, your sins are forgiven" (v 33).

Jesus says he'll forgive the man—forgive him for all the ways he's ignored God and rejected his friendship and decided to do things his own way instead.

But, hang on—who said anything about any of that?

It's not hard to imagine the man's reaction: *Um... thanks, Jesus. But that's not why I came. In case you haven't noticed, I've got bigger problems here!*

But actually, that's not true. This guy's legs *aren't* his biggest problem. Sure, walking will make him happy for a while. But the crowd around him is full of tired, unhappy people with two working legs.

Jesus knows the man needs more. He needs the same thing as the rest of the crowd. He needs the same thing we *all* need. This man doesn't just need a miracle from God. He needs a way back into God's kingdom.

Because friendship with God is what the man was made for. Nothing else will make him truly, forever happy.

Thankfully, this is exactly what Jesus' good news is all about!

Jesus is here to forgive sin. He's here to fix what's broken between people and God.

What do you think of the idea that restoring your friendship with God is Jesus' number one priority for your life?

PRAYER

Dear God, thank you that Jesus' good news is way bigger than just healing injuries and diseases. Thank you that Jesus came to fix what's broken between people and God. Please help me, more and more, to understand what that means for me. Amen.

⚑ DAY 13 ⚑

WHO CAN FORGIVE?

READ MARK 2 v 5-12

Imagine you're hanging out with two friends. Out of nowhere, one of them comes up and punches you on the nose. But then, as you stagger back, clutching your face, your other friend turns to the one who hit you and says, "Don't worry about it. I forgive you."

What's your reaction?

"*What?* What do you mean *you* forgive them? *You're* not the one who got punched in the face! You don't get to forgive them! Only *I* get to decide that!"

Here, Jesus gets a similar reaction from some religious leaders.

Standing over the paralysed man, he says, "Son, your sins are forgiven" (v 5).

And then, across the room, he spots a bunch of faces looking *furious* at what he's just said.

Who does Jesus think he is? "Sin" is pushing *God* aside. It's turning away from *God*. How can *Jesus* claim to forgive this man's sins? Only *God* gets to do that!

Jesus' response is incredible. Basically, he says, *You're right. Only God can forgive sins. But you know what else only God can do?* And he turns back to the paralysed man and says, *Get up and walk.*

And the man gets up and walks.

The crowd is stunned—and not just by the miracle.

Because if Jesus can do the impossible thing they *can* see, what does that say about the impossible thing they *can't* see?

Only God can forgive sin. So if *Jesus* can forgive sin...

What does that tell us about who Jesus really is?

PRAYER

Dear God, thank you that Jesus didn't just come here to *talk* about forgiving sins, but that he came here with the power and authority to actually *do* it. As I keep reading through Mark, please help me see how Jesus came to deal with *my* sin too. Amen.

⚒ DAY 14 ⚒

GOOD GUYS, BAD GUYS?

READ MARK 2 v 13-17

Jesus is having dinner with Levi the tax collector and a bunch of his friends. The religious leaders burst in and see what's going on... and they're shocked and confused.

Why?

A bit of history: in 63 BC, Israel (the homeland of God's people) was invaded by the Roman general Pompey and his armies.

Fast-forward 90-ish years to Levi's dinner party, and the Romans are *still* running the show.

God's people aren't slaves exactly, but they're not free either. And one of the *big* reminders of this is the regular tax which the Roman Empire demands from all its people.

Except the Romans don't collect this tax themselves. They hire locals to do it. If you're a tax collector, your job is to go to your *own people*, take their money, and give it to the empire. Even worse, many of these tax collectors take more than they are supposed to and keep the extra for themselves.

Tax collectors were traitors and thieves. Which explains the Pharisees' question: *if Jesus is a good guy, why is he hanging out with the bad guys?*

In response, Jesus starts talking about doctors. Like a doctor, Jesus has come to bring healing. But as we've seen, he's here to fix more than just bodies. He's here to bring forgiveness to people who are far from God. That's what's on offer to *anyone* who accepts Jesus' invitation and follows him (v 14).

So *of course* Jesus is hanging out with the bad guys! That's exactly who he's here to help!

But as we'll soon see, the "tax collectors and sinners" aren't the only ones in the room who need Jesus' help...

Do you ever worry that you might be too bad for God to give you a fresh start? What do you think Jesus would have to say about that?

PRAYER

Dear God, when I feel far away from you, remind me that Jesus came to give a fresh start to sinners, traitors and thieves. Thank you that, in Jesus, you offer me a fresh start too, again and again, as often as I need it. Amen.

DAY 15

CELEBRATION TIME!

READ MARK 2 v 18-22

Yesterday, we saw Jesus comparing himself to a doctor. This time, it's a groom at a wedding.

More and more people are watching Jesus, and some are wondering why his followers aren't fasting like the followers of John the Baptist or the Pharisees.

Fasting is going without food for a while as a way to focus your attention on seeking God. It was common in Israel in the time of Jesus, and many people still fast today.

Fasting was often associated with sadness—Israel were God's people, but now their land had been invaded, and they felt far from God. They were hoping and praying for things to be made right again.

But if there was one place where they wouldn't *dream* of fasting, it was a wedding. Weddings in first-century Israel were giant, week-long, whole-town celebrations! Who could possibly fast in the middle of all that joy?

And so when Jesus is asked why his disciples aren't fasting, he compares his arrival to the start of a wedding.

(This, by the way, is another huge hint about who Jesus is, because centuries earlier *God himself* had talked about being like a husband for his people—someone who was committed to his people and promised to love them, no matter what.)

Now isn't a time for fasting, Jesus says. *It's a time for celebration!*

Why? Because, in Jesus, God is doing something brand new—something that demands a brand new response (which is what Jesus is getting at in verses 21-22).

In Jesus, everything the Pharisees have been hoping and praying for is standing right here in front of them.

In Jesus, God himself has come near.

What's the biggest party you've ever been to? What have you read in Mark's Gospel that has helped you get excited about Jesus' arrival?

PRAYER

Lord, thank you for loving your people even better than the best husband-to-be loves his bride. In a world filled with such joy and such sadness, please keep helping me to understand all that Jesus came to do for us. Help me to be thankful and celebrate. Amen.

⊠ DAY 16 ⊠
REAL REST

READ MARK 2 v 23-28

If you had the whole day off tomorrow to rest, how would you spend it?

In Israel, a rest day wasn't just a nice idea. Centuries earlier, God had put it in their law: every Saturday, *everyone* had to take a Sabbath—a day off to rest and remember God's goodness. At that time, God had just rescued his people from slavery in Egypt. For 400 years, they'd been told that their only value came from how much they worked.

The Sabbath was a weekly opportunity to refocus on God and remember the truth: that they were infinitely valuable, not because of anything they *did* but simply because they were God's beloved children.

But fast-forward to Jesus' day, and the Pharisees have invented so many add-on rules about what technically counts as "resting" that they've turned the Sabbath into the hardest work day of the week!

For example, obviously harvesting your field counts as work. But many Pharisees wouldn't even *look in the mirror* on the Sabbath, because what if you see an out-of-place hair and you pluck it out? Wouldn't that technically count as *harvesting*? (If you think this sounds extreme, you're right.)

So anyway, when the Pharisees catch Jesus' disciples picking themselves a snack on the way through a cornfield, they're outraged. These guys are breaking the rules! They're *harvesting*!

But Jesus says they're missing the point. In all their rule-keeping, they've forgotten what the Sabbath is all about: turning back to God and resting in his love (v 27).

Jesus, the Son of Man, is Lord of the Sabbath.

And in God's kingdom, there is rest and refreshment for everyone.

Are you ever tempted to believe that your value or importance comes from what you do? When? How could you remind yourself of the truth?

PRAYER

Loving God, my life feels so busy sometimes, but you say rest is just as important as work. Thank you for the gift of rest. Please help me to take regular time out to rest and remind myself of your love. Amen.

★ ◢ DAY 17 ◣
LOOKING FOR ★
EXCUSES
★

READ MARK 3 v 1-6

In today's reading, Jesus has another run-in with the Pharisees. By now they aren't just questioning Jesus—they're looking for reasons to accuse him.

At this point, you might be wondering, "Who *are* these guys, anyway? Why are they so obsessed with Jesus?"

Well, as we've seen, when the Romans conquered Israel, some Israelites (like the tax collectors) responded by going to work for the enemy.

The Pharisees had the completely opposite response. Instead of blending in with Rome, they wanted to be *different*—to devote their lives to God by following his law.

But the Pharisees didn't stop with God's rules. They kept inventing their own extra rules *about* God's rules. Rules like not looking in the mirror on the Sabbath. Rules they said everyone *else* had to follow too, if they wanted God to have anything to do with them.

Eventually, they became so focused on *rule-keeping* that they forgot what God's law was really all about: loving God and loving other people.

And so, here in the synagogue, Jesus calls them out.

He takes a moment on the Sabbath to heal and bring life—and lets the Pharisees' reaction show what they *really* care about.

They say they're devoted to God. But now God is doing something extraordinary right in front of them, and they're completely missing it. The Pharisees aren't interested in God's kingdom. They're not interested in life and healing. They're just interested in their own power and rules.

And so they close their hearts to Jesus and start plotting to kill him.

As we read Mark's Gospel, what's your reaction to Jesus so far? Are there any particular areas where you need to open your heart to hear what he has to say?

PRAYER

Loving God, please help me to keep an open heart and an open mind about everything I'm reading in Mark's Gospel. Please keep me from being like the Pharisees, who turned away from the truth that was right in front of them. Please show me who you really are. Amen.

⚑ DAY 18 ⚑

WHOSE MISSION?

★ READ MARK 3 v 7-12

Have you ever been in a crowd so packed that you worried you might get trampled?

As Jesus' popularity skyrockets, that's exactly where he finds himself. These aren't just local crowds anymore—there are people here from a hundred miles away! And they're so desperate to reach Jesus that he has to escape in a boat to avoid getting crushed.

But most of this crowd isn't here to hear about God's kingdom or get on board with Jesus' mission.

They're here to get Jesus on board with *their* mission: they want to be healed!

But being healed will only make them happy for today. It won't keep them safe for tomorrow. Jesus has a bigger, better mission. And the more the crowds misunderstand that mission, the harder it is for Jesus to keep it moving forward.

Which is why, whenever a spirit shouts out Jesus' *true* identity, he tells it to keep quiet. It's only trying to make things worse.

Yes, Jesus is the one God's people have been waiting for—the promised rescuer, like their great king David from long ago. But Jesus' rescue will look nothing like they imagine.

David was a military king who drove Israel's enemies from their land with his powerful armies. And that's exactly the sort of Messiah most of the people are hoping for now.

Again, the people are looking for someone to get on board with *their* mission. They want someone to raise up an army to drive out the Romans!

But again, Jesus has a bigger, better mission. He's not just here to free the people from sickness or from the empire. He's here to free them from death itself.

As you investigate Jesus, are you hoping to get on board with his mission or to get him on board with yours? How can you tell the difference?

PRAYER

Father, I'm sorry for when I've wanted you to get on board with how I want things. Help me to see how Jesus' mission is bigger and better than any plans for my life that I could invent on my own. Help me to understand what Jesus' mission is and to be excited about getting on board. Amen.

⬢ DAY 19 ⬢

THE NEW TWELVE

READ MARK 3 v 13-19

How much do you know about your family history? What about the history of your country?

For God's people in Israel, those two questions were actually the *same* question. The nation of Israel was named after a *person* called Israel (aka Jacob), whose twelve sons became the ancestors of Israel's twelve tribes. After freeing them from slavery in Egypt, God brought these twelve tribes to a mountain and gave them a mission: to follow him and invite others to do the same.

And so, centuries later, when Jesus brings twelve Israelite men to a mountain and gives them a mission to follow him and invite others to do the same, he's making a point.

Once again, Jesus is rewriting the story of God's people.

All through their history, the twelve tribes of Israel *failed* in their mission and became just like everyone else, ignoring and forgetting and rejecting God.

But now here's Jesus, appointing a *new* twelve.

To be honest, though, they're not exactly impressive. Jesus' twelve disciples are a bunch of uneducated fishermen, tax collectors, rebels, traitors and thieves. If these guys are meant to be the great shining hope of God's kingdom, this mission seems doomed from the start.

But look closely at verse 14: what's the *first* thing Jesus calls his new twelve to do?

It's to *be with him*.

Jesus isn't appointing these guys because they have what it takes. He's appointing them because *he* has what it takes.

And in Greek (the language Mark originally wrote in), that word "appointed" is actually the same as "created"—a word describing an artist making a beautiful piece of art.

Jesus isn't just *calling* these guys. He's *creating* them into the people they were always meant to be.

Do you ever feel like you need to do or be something to impress God? What do you think Jesus would say about this?

PRAYER

Father, thank you that you don't call me to be impressive; you just call me to be with you. Please keep speaking to me as I read the Bible, and keep changing me into the person you made me to be. Amen.

SEEING CLEARLY

★ **READ MARK 3 v 20-30**

Imagine hearing that your own brother is suddenly attracting huge crowds of people wherever he goes—and that he's convincing those crowds that he can do miracles and that he's been sent by God as their rescuing hero.

What would your reaction be?

For Jesus' family, the answer is simple: *our brother's gone crazy. He's out of his mind!* (v 21).

And they're not the only ones who say something's not right. Israel's leaders are still looking for a way to get rid of Jesus.

They'd love for the crowds to just *ignore* him, but that won't work because they've all *seen* the incredible power he has.

The leaders can't dispute his power. So, instead, they dispute the *source* of that power: *He hasn't been sent by God! He's been sent by God's enemy* (v 22).

Jesus asks the obvious question (v 23-27): if he's working for the dark side, why on earth is he driving out the forces of darkness and leading people back to God? Why would God's enemy be working against himself?

The leaders' claim doesn't match up with the evidence. But then, these guys haven't been seeing the evidence clearly for a while now.

Both Israel's leaders and Jesus' own family are making the same mistake. Instead of taking a clear look at Jesus' life and letting *that* guide their thinking, they've closed their minds to the evidence and come up with a story to fit what they've already decided to believe.

In verse 29, Jesus warns them of the danger of this way of thinking; he's here on a mission of healing and forgiveness. What he's doing isn't the work of God's enemy but of God's own Holy Spirit. Anyone who rejects Jesus is rejecting the forgiveness God sent him to bring.

What opinions do you already have that might keep you from seeing Jesus clearly?

PRAYER

Loving Father, please help me to see Jesus clearly. May I be convinced not by my own opinions or the kind of background I come from but by the evidence of Jesus' own life. Amen.

✄ DAY 21 ✄
MY BROTHER, THE MESSIAH

READ MARK 3 v 31-35

Imagine you're Jesus' brother James. You've grown up with Jesus. You've known him your whole life. But now he's going around, acting as if he's God's promised Messiah. He even says he can forgive sins.

Clearly, he's lost his mind.

So you and your family go to the place where he's staying. If you can just get him away from the crowds, maybe you can talk some sense into him.

But when you get to the house, he won't even come out to see you. Worse still, he starts talking like you guys aren't even his true family. He says *his* real brother and sister and mother is whoever does God's will.

Which is what, exactly?

Well, obviously, there's the law that God gave your ancestors.

But when Jesus talks about God's will, he seems to be talking about something bigger and deeper than just obeying God's rules—something connected to Jesus himself and to this kingdom he keeps talking about.

According to Jesus, God's will is for people to "repent and believe the good news!" (1 v 15). Jesus says that anyone who puts their trust in *him* can be part of God's family.

If you were James, Jesus' brother, how easy would it be to believe all this?

Impossible, maybe. But then, impossible isn't a problem for God.

We know from history that James ended up realising the truth about his brother. He became a follower of Jesus and even wrote a book of the Bible (it's called James!).

He spent the rest of his life inviting others to do what he'd done: to repent and believe the good news. To be welcomed home to God's family. And to hold on to the truth about who Jesus is, even if everyone else thinks we're out of our minds.

Is there anyone you know who would think you were out of your mind for following Jesus? What difference does it make to know that you can be part of Jesus' family?

PRAYER

Father, thank you that you invite everyone, everywhere, to turn back to you and become part of your family. Please help me understand what this means for me. Amen.

⚔ DAY 22 ⚔

LETTING JESUS SPEAK FOR HIMSELF

★ READ MARK 4 v 1-9 ★

Have you ever been in a situation where you had people talking about you or assuming things about you without actually letting you speak for yourself?

At the shore of Lake Galilee, another huge crowd has gathered around Jesus and, as usual, it's filled with all kinds of people.

People like the Pharisees and teachers, who think Jesus is a dangerous threat. People like Jesus' family, who think he's out of his mind. People pushing forward to receive a healing—or maybe just to see a healing. People who want Jesus to grab a sword and lead the charge against the Romans.

But how many of these people are actually willing to let Jesus speak for himself?

Sitting in the boat, Jesus begins to teach.

There was a farmer. He scattered seed in different places. Different things happened to it. If you've got ears, listen.

What is Jesus doing here? Why is he suddenly handing out farming tips?

Mark lets us in on the answer: he's using a parable—a made-up image or story with a real-world meaning.

Jesus is talking about a farmer sowing seed, but he's actually talking about the kingdom of God and how people respond to it. He's talking about seed and soil, but he's actually talking about the crowd in front of him.

But what's funny is that he doesn't stop to explain this to them—at least, not yet. He just leaves them wondering, *What on earth was that about?*

Which is exactly the point. This crowd has plenty of opinions about Jesus. But how many of them care enough to really consider what Jesus has to say? How many of them care enough to stick around and ask questions?

Are you getting your beliefs about Jesus from the crowd around you or are you listening to what he's actually saying?

PRAYER

Loving God, in a world full of opinions about who you are, please help me to clearly hear what you have to say about yourself. Help me understand who you really are. Amen.

✠ DAY 23 ✠

THE SECRET OF THE KINGDOM

READ MARK 4 v 10-12

Have you ever had a teacher who seemed to make things confusing on purpose?

Doesn't it seem like that's what Jesus is doing here?

First, he shares this parable about seed, which he doesn't even explain. And then, when his disciples ask about it, Jesus says he teaches in parables *so that* people might keep seeing and hearing him but not understand him—otherwise they might turn and be forgiven!

What's Jesus saying? That he *wants* to be misunderstood? That he wants to *stop* people turning back to God for forgiveness? Hasn't he been saying all along that helping people find forgiveness is the whole reason he's here?

What on earth is going on?

Well, Jesus isn't just pulling these words out of nowhere. He's quoting Isaiah the prophet, who spoke them to Israel

700 years earlier. It was a dark time in Israel's history. God's people had rejected God so completely and for so long that they'd closed their hearts and minds to what God had to say to them.

It wasn't that they *couldn't* understand if they tried. It was that they'd given up trying.

And Jesus says something similar is going on here. He isn't *stopping* anyone from understanding him—Jesus only ever taught people "as much as they could understand" (Mark 4 v 33).

The problem is that people have already given up trying.

They're too busy *telling* Jesus who he is to hear who he *actually* is.

But for anyone who genuinely wants to know, Jesus' parables are an open invitation to discover what the secret of God's kingdom is all about (v 11). But first, they'll need to stop and listen—to ask questions and stick around long enough to hear the answers.

What questions do you still have about Jesus? Where are you looking for answers?

PRAYER

Loving Father, as I investigate Jesus, please keep my heart and mind open to everything you have to teach me. Please keep guiding me towards the truth about who you are. Amen.

MIXED RESPONSES

★ **READ MARK 4 v 13-20** ★

By now, the crowds have gone home, and Jesus is back on shore. All that's left are his disciples and the few others interested enough to stick around and ask questions.

They ask about the parable, and Jesus answers.

The farmer is Jesus. The seed is the good news of God's kingdom. And the different places where the seed lands are different people's reactions to that good news.

Some hear Jesus' message and immediately reject it. We've seen this reaction from the Pharisees and teachers. If anyone was going to be excited about Jesus, it should've been them. But Jesus doesn't play by their rules, so they've rejected him without even hearing him out.

Other people are excited about Jesus at first, but their excitement is only surface-deep. We've seen this from people in the crowds who just want healing, or a show, or an army commander. Really, they just want Jesus to get on board with what *they're* doing. And so when trouble comes—when following Jesus takes too much effort or when Jesus doesn't do what they want—they bail.

The third group seem like they really care about Jesus. The problem is that they care more about other things. They want Jesus, but they want money more. Or popularity. Or some other achievement. And so they chase off after those other things and forget Jesus.

The truth is, none of these people actually want Jesus.

They just want to use Jesus to get what they *really* want.

But then there's a fourth group of people who actually stop and listen to Jesus. They hear the good news. They repent and believe. And they step into the abundant, overflowing life of the kingdom of God.

Which of these responses to Jesus do you most identify with? Which response do you think Jesus deserves?

PRAYER

Loving God, please help me to see how following Jesus is better than any other dream or goal I could chase after, and is worth it even when it's tough. Thank you that Jesus' good news is good news for me. Amen.

⚑ DAY 25 ⚑

A LAMP ON A STAND

READ MARK 4 v 21-25

Imagine you're at home one night when, suddenly, the power goes out in your street. You feel your way into the next room, fumble through your drawer, find a torch, switch it on...

And immediately shut the torch back inside the drawer.

Doesn't make much sense, does it?

The whole point of a torch is to light up the darkness. No one turns on a light just to hide it away again!

And Jesus says the same thing is true of God's kingdom.

Jesus' message is a blazing torch, lighting up the darkness of the world. It's brilliant, bright, life-changing, life-*saving* news! Who in their right mind would hide something like that away?

Jesus has been talking about the "secret" of the kingdom— but the news that we can enjoy living with God as our King isn't meant to be *kept* secret. It's meant to be brought out into the open, where it can drive out the darkness in every direction!

And so the question isn't "Does Jesus want to be known?"

It's "Do you want to know him?"

If you have a good and loyal friend, then the more you put into that friendship—the more you listen to them, talk to them, spend time with them—the closer and stronger that friendship will grow.

And the same goes for Jesus and his kingdom message: "With the measure you use, it will be measured to you—and even more" (v 24).

In other words, if you insist on ignoring the good news, you'll end up missing out on the whole thing.

But the more you listen to Jesus—the more you ask for his help to keep getting to know him and the more closely you follow him—the more life and light and joy you'll find.

What's one thing you could do today to work on your friendship with Jesus?

PRAYER

Loving God, thank you for coming to earth as Jesus so that I can truly understand who you are. I want to listen. Please help me to keep on getting to know you better every day. Amen.

✦ ✪ DAY 26 ✪

IT'S KIND OF ✪ LIKE THIS

✪
READ MARK 4 v 26-34

Imagine trying to describe the internet to someone living a thousand years ago.

They wouldn't know what photos or videos are. They've never seen a computer, or a phone, or anything that runs on electricity.

How do you explain something so completely different to anything they've ever seen before?

If you just *told* them what it was, they wouldn't understand.

Instead, you'd probably find yourself saying things like, "Well, it's kind of like this..."

As Jesus teaches about God's kingdom, he's in a similar situation. This new life that he's come to invite us into is so huge, so incredible, so *different* to anything we've seen before that he can't just *tell* us what it is in a sentence.

Instead, he says, *God's kingdom is kind of like this...*

It's like seed scattered onto different soils, because different people respond to it in different ways (v 14-20).

It's like a lamp, because it's meant to be seen and understood—and because it drives away the darkness (v 21-23).

It's like a seed growing by day and night, because it doesn't depend on human power to flourish (v 26-29).

It's like a mustard seed, because it seems insignificant, almost *invisible*, at first—but it will grow to fill the whole earth (v 30-32).

And it's like a whole bunch of other things too. No single parable gives us the *full* picture of God's kingdom, but by putting them all together, we can start to see more clearly what Jesus' good news is all about.

But Jesus didn't just describe God's kingdom with words. He also showed it through his actions—and that's exactly what Mark is going to tell us about next!

Based on everything you've read so far, how would you describe God's kingdom?

PRAYER

Dear God, thank you for inviting me into a kingdom so huge and amazing that I can hardly wrap my mind around it. Help me not to be frustrated by what I don't yet understand, but to trust you to keep showing yourself to me, one step at a time. Amen.

☒ DAY 27 ☒

DON'T YOU CARE?

READ MARK 4 v 35-39

At over 200 metres (650 feet) below sea level, the Sea of Galilee is the world's lowest freshwater lake. Cold winds blow in regularly from the Mediterranean Sea, rushing down between the mountains, whipping up huge storms on the water.

This isn't news to Jesus' friends. Simon, Andrew, James and John are experienced fishermen. They've spent countless hours on this lake. They know how rough the waters can get out here.

But whatever storms they've been through before, this one is worse. The situation is completely out of their control.

And in the middle of it all, Jesus is sleeping.

His friends jolt him awake: "Don't you care if we drown?" (v 38). Jesus gets up, and he answers his friends in about the most dramatic way possible.

Not only does Jesus care but he's powerful to help—so powerful that "even the wind and the waves obey him" (v 41)!

But remember, Jesus never does stuff like this just to show off his power. His miracles are all about showing us more of who he is and what God's kingdom is all about.

In this case, Jesus' message is loud and clear: *Chaos and fear have no place in my kingdom.*

One day, when God's kingdom comes in all its fullness, chaos and fear will be completely wiped off the face of the earth.

In the meantime, though, when we suffer, it can be easy to ask the same question that Jesus' friends asked: *Does God even care? Is he even out there?*

Jesus is God's ultimate answer to those questions. And as we keep reading, we'll see just how far Jesus was willing to go to come to our rescue.

Do you ever doubt God's love for you? What do you think Jesus would say about those doubts?

PRAYER

Dear God, thank you for this incredible glimpse of your power—and that you've promised to one day wipe out all chaos and fear forever. In the meantime, help me to trust that you are in control and that you love me. Amen.

⚑ DAY 28 ⚑

WHY ARE YOU SO AFRAID? ★

READ MARK 4 v 40

What's the most scared you've ever been? For Jesus' disciples, this night out on the lake had to be up there with the most terrifying moments of their lives.

But now, in an instant, everything around them has changed.

The waves have died down. The winds have blown themselves out. The sky is suddenly, unnervingly clear. The friends stare around in shock—until the eerie silence is broken by a question from Jesus: "Why are you so afraid?" (v 40).

Which seems like a weird thing to ask, right?

Of course we're afraid! We almost died!

But the second half of Jesus' question helps explain the first. "Do you still have no faith?"

Or, in other words, *Don't you trust me?*

And Jesus isn't just saying, *You can relax now. The danger has passed.*

He's saying they *never* had to be afraid—not even while the storm was still raging.

Because Jesus' friends weren't just in a storm back there. They were in a storm *with Jesus*. And remembering that would have made all the difference.

As long as they focused on the storm, of course they'd be scared! The storm was way too big for them. But if they'd focused on Jesus, they would've realised that they didn't need to be afraid, because the storm wasn't too big for him.

And in dark, scary times in our own lives, Jesus offers us the same choice. We can focus on our fear—or we can focus on Jesus and remind ourselves that he's in control, even when we're not.

How do you usually respond when things feel out of your control? How would remembering that Jesus is in control help you to see your situation differently?

PRAYER

Mighty God, when it feels like my life is spinning out of control, remind me that being in control isn't actually my job—it's yours. Help me to trust in your love for me, and let that bring me peace on the inside, even when life is chaotic on the outside. Amen.

⧓ DAY 29 ⧓

WHO IS THIS ★ MAN?

READ MARK 4 v 41

We've seen before how people in the ancient world used the raging sea to describe situations of darkness, chaos and fear.

On page 1 of the Bible, the author describes God's Spirit hovering over the waters—over the dark, chaotic nothingness before creation.

But then God speaks—and light floods into the darkness.

Who is God? What is he like?

God is the one who brings light to the darkness. God is the one who brings order to the chaos. God is the one who brings peace to the fear. God is powerful. He's in control. He can be trusted.

Fast-forward to Jesus' friends, caught in an actual, literal raging sea that's turned their whole world dark and terrifying.

But then Jesus speaks—and light floods into the darkness.

The storm stops.

Jesus' friends turn to each other, more freaked out than ever. How on earth are they meant to explain what they've just witnessed? "Who *is* this man?"

But right here, Jesus has given them another huge clue to his true identity—because there's only one person in existence with this kind of power.

The same God who spoke light into the darkness in the very beginning is right there with them in their boat, doing what he's been doing all along—bringing light to the darkness, order to the chaos, peace to the fear.

In the middle of their suffering and despair, in the deepest darkness, when all hope seemed lost, where was God?

He was right there with them, willing and able to bring them safely through the storm and out the other side.

If Jesus really was the God of the universe here on earth as a human being, what does that tell us about what God is like?

PRAYER

Dear God, thank you that, whatever storms I might face, you promise to be right beside me, guiding me through them. Thank you that Jesus has power over every situation. Please help me to understand what it looks like to trust in him. Amen.

⚞ DAY 30 ⚟ ✶

INVISIBLE EVIL

✶ ✶

READ MARK 5 V 1-6

At last, Jesus' disciples make it back to land. But that raging storm isn't the only force of chaos in their path.

A man charges down from the tombs, dirty and ragged, covered in sores. He's being haunted by an impure spirit (or *spirits*, actually, as we'll see).

These things can't hurt God directly—he's far too powerful. Instead, they attack what God loves most in the whole universe: us.

And so here's this man whose whole life has been reduced to ruins by the forces of darkness. Instead of experiencing the love and freedom he was created for, he's been driven from his home, separated from his family and imprisoned by powers he can't control. It's a heartbreaking picture.

And *weird*, right?

What should we make of all this talk about invisible spirits? Is there really any such thing?

Some people say this is all just superstitious nonsense, from back before people understood about psychology and medicine and mental illness.

But the truth is that the Bible regularly describes people whose minds are troubled or unwell *without* bringing impure spirits into it. The writers knew the difference. So this isn't superstition; it's a whole other thing.

The Bible's view of reality isn't shallower or less educated than the views we're used to hearing. It's deeper and wiser and more complex, because it recognises something we usually ignore.

Yes, people are responsible for so much of the evil and brokenness in the world. But behind all that *visible* evil lies something else—something mysterious and *invisible* that connects with our world in ways we don't always understand.

But Mark's point in recounting these events isn't to freak us out about dark spiritual forces. It's to remind us that those forces are no match for the love and power of Jesus.

Does this story challenge the way you usually think about the world? How?

PRAYER

God, as I consider these claims about spiritual forces, help me not to be either closed-minded or fearful, but to trust that your love is bigger and stronger than anything else in the universe. Amen.

DAY 31
LEGION

READ MARK 5 v 7-13

What's the scariest movie you've ever seen? Here among the tombs, Jesus and his friends encounter something that feels torn straight from a horror movie— except that the darkness overtaking this man is all too real.

The spirits have twisted his mind to breaking point. They've filled his body with monstrous strength, but only so he can more brutally hurt himself and anyone who tries to help him.

They've made it their mission to steal his humanity. But Jesus won't have it. He knows the man is still in there. He asks him for his name.

But when the reply comes, it's clearly not the man who's answering.

The spirits move the man's lips, speaking with the man's voice: "My name is Legion ... for we are many" (v 9).

In the Roman army, a legion was made up of six thousand men. This man isn't just *haunted* by spirits. He's *infested* with them: completely outnumbered and overpowered.

Just as with the storm, this situation seems utterly hopeless. But just as with the storm, all Jesus has to do is speak, and the darkness has no choice but to flee.

The spirits evacuate into a herd of pigs and, suddenly, the hillside echoes with scrabbling hooves and blood-chilling squeals as two thousand bodies go crashing to their deaths in the lake.

It's a nightmarish scene—a senseless display of the spirits' violence and destruction. But when the dust settles, the spirits are gone.

And by freeing this one man from their control, Jesus gives us a glimpse of the ultimate fate of *all* the forces of evil. God's kingdom is a place of peace, wholeness and freedom—and one day, when Jesus brings that kingdom in all its fullness, the powers of darkness will be driven out forever.

Where do you see evil in the world today? How might trusting that Jesus will one day defeat all evil change the way you live, here and now?

PRAYER

God, when I feel anxious about the evil in the world, please remind me that things won't always be this way. Help me to trust in your power and your love. Amen.

FOR EVERYONE

READ MARK 5 v 14-20

Imagine you're a pig-herder, standing on a hillside, minding your boss's pigs.

Some men arrive in a boat. They're from way across the lake, which means they're probably Israelites—foreigners who don't follow your customs or worship your gods.

As you watch, they're met by that miserable guy who lives in the tombs. One of the Israelites steps forward, speaking to the man full of spirits... And the hillside erupts in chaos.

The pigs you're meant to be guarding lose their minds and stampede into the lake. You race into town, wondering what on earth to tell your boss.

When you return, things get even weirder. Because there's the guy from the tombs, dressed and completely calm.

How do you react?

As usual, Mark records vastly different responses to Jesus.

Most of the town want Jesus *gone*. Clearly he's unsafe. But the man from the tombs has seen Jesus' goodness first-hand. He begs to join him.

But Jesus has a different mission for the man: *Go tell your people what I've done for you* (v 19).

Usually in Mark's Gospel, this is where Jesus tells whoever he's just helped to keep quiet. But over here, it's different. These people aren't Israelites. They won't try to make Jesus their military Messiah, because they don't even know there's a Messiah coming.

So the man travels through the Decapolis (the Ten Cities), sharing the story of Jesus' mercy to him, and all the people are amazed.

Meanwhile, by travelling into this foreign territory to help someone who isn't even one of his own people, Jesus shows us something else: yes, Jesus is the Messiah Israel has been waiting for, but he hasn't just come to save Israel.

God's kingdom isn't just open to *one* kind of person. This good news is for everyone.

How do you think you'd respond if you saw something like this with your own eyes?

PRAYER

Father, thank you that Jesus' good news is for everyone. Please help me to see how it's good news for me, and to share that good news with others. Amen.

⚡ DAY 33 ⚡
HURRY!

READ MARK 5 v 21-30

Think of a time when you've been in a *desperate* hurry. You had to act *quickly*, or everything would fall apart.

Jairus hears that Jesus is back in town. He jolts into action. This is it: his last hope.

He fights through the crowd, crashing at Jesus' feet.

"My little daughter is dying!"

Jesus says he'll help, and Jairus sets off at a run—or tries to, anyway. Crushed by the crowd, they can barely walk.

Panic twists Jairus' insides. What's everybody's *problem*? Why won't they *move*?

And then things go from bad to worse. A sick woman touches Jesus' cloak, and instantly she's well. But instead of pushing on towards Jairus' house, Jesus stops. He searches the crowd, looking for whoever he's just healed.

Seriously?

A girl is dying, and Jesus thinks he's got time to stop for a chat?

But Jesus won't be hurried. He knows what he's doing. He's said he'll save Jairus' daughter, and he will. Jairus, his daughter, and this sick woman will *all* get way more than they imagine from Jesus. And, painful as it is, even the waiting is part of God's kindness to them.

The same is true for us. Jesus *always* does what he says he'll do—but often not as quickly as we'd like.

Sometimes that waiting feels unbearable, like God is uncaring, or cruel, or not even there. But, as with Jairus, if God makes us wait, it's only ever because he's got a bigger, better plan.

If you expect God to stick to your timetable, you'll often wind up disappointed. But the more you trust him to keep his promises, even when it takes longer than you'd like, the more you'll be blown away by his mercy and love.

How easy do you find it to wait for God to answer your prayers? Have you ever been in a situation where God did something bigger and better than you expected?

PRAYER

Father, when it feels like you're taking *forever* to help, help me trust that you have a bigger, better plan than I can see, and that even the waiting is part of your kindness to me. Amen.

⮚ DAY 34 ⮘

⭑ TOTAL ⭑ TRANSFORMATION

⭑ READ MARK 5 v 30-34

While Jairus worries for his daughter, a woman presses through the crowd. She's been sick for twelve years. She's lost all her money. Most people assume that she's been cursed by God. Why else would she have stayed sick all this time?

She knows she's not meant to be here. No one in her condition should be touching all these other people. The law says she shouldn't even be out in public without loudly warning everyone that she's unclean.

But she stretches forward. Her fingers brush Jesus' cloak. And immediately, she's healed.

She backs away quietly, thinking no one realises what's happened. She's got what she thinks she needs, and now she just wants to be left alone.

But Jesus loves her too much for that. He doesn't just want to heal her sickness. He wants to free her from the rumours about being cursed. He wants to reunite her with her community. He wants to know her and hear her story. He wants to bring health and healing to every part of her life.

So he stops. He calls her forward. And it's scary, and uncomfortable, and everyone's staring at her, but by getting her up in front of all her neighbours, he's announcing publicly that she's healed and clean and loved by God.

The experience of getting healed by Jesus turns out to be harder and more confronting than she expected, but in the end, Jesus sends her away with what she hasn't had in twelve years: peace and freedom.

And Jesus wants the same for you. He loves you way too much to just give you what you think you need and then leave you alone.

Jesus hasn't come to just help you along a bit. He's come to transform your whole life from the inside out.

What areas of your life might need transformation? How comfortable are you with the idea that Jesus wants to help you change?

PRAYER

Lord God, you want to transform me into the person I was always meant to be—which will sometimes mean taking me out of my comfort zone. Help me see this for what it is: another sign of your love and care for me. Amen.

⚑ DAY 35 ⚑ ★

WHEN THE WORST HAPPENS

★ **READ MARK 5 v 35-36** ★

Imagine a doctor working in a hospital emergency room. Two patients are rushed through the doors at the same time.

The first is a young girl. She needs urgent help in the next few minutes, or she'll die. The second is an older woman who's been sick for years. It won't make much difference whether the doctor gets to her in five minutes or five weeks.

The doctor examines the two patients, thinks for a moment... and then, apparently in no hurry at all, he turns to help the older woman.

What would you say about a doctor like this?

A while back, Jesus compared himself to a doctor. But any doctor who made decisions like this today would probably be sent to prison!

How must Jairus be feeling right now?

This is *exactly* why he had been so urgent. But instead of hurrying to Jairus' daughter, Jesus has just wasted her dying moments on some woman who wasn't even that sick!

And now Jairus' daughter is dead. It's over.

Does Jesus even care?

Jesus hears the news, and he turns to Jairus with the same reassurance he had for his disciples in the storm.

You don't need to be afraid. You need to trust me. Will you do that? Will you keep trusting me, even now?

It seems that all hope is lost. But with Jesus, that's absolutely never true.

The trouble isn't a sign that Jesus doesn't care. The trouble isn't a sign that Jesus has got it wrong.

The trouble is an opportunity to trust Jesus, even when things seem completely hopeless and out of control—because, with Jesus, there's always more to the story.

When things go wrong, how easy do you find it to believe that God is trustworthy and kind? How could remembering this story help?

PRAYER

Loving God, when things feel hopeless, when it feels like everything is going wrong, please help me to trust that you are in control, that you love me, and that there's always more to the story than I can see. Amen.

★ ⚑ DAY 36 ⚑

TWIST ENDING

READ MARK 5 v 37-43 ★

If you turn off a movie twenty minutes before the end, and then complain that it didn't answer all your questions... that's probably not the moviemaker's fault.

Often, it's the end of the story that explains the rest.

So far, to Jairus, Jesus must seem completely unreasonable, even heartless. But here at the end comes a twist that makes sense of everything.

Jesus holds back the crowd for this part, but he brings three disciples along. He wants them to see this. Reaching the house, Jesus says he's here to wake up Jairus' daughter. Unsurprisingly, this announcement is met by shocked, disbelieving laughter. Is this guy insane or just cruel?

But Jesus takes the dead girl gently by the hand: *Honey, it's time to wake up.* And instantly, all Jairus' anger and confusion vanishes, and it's replaced by awe and wonder and tears of joy.

She's alive!

Here is the ending that makes sense of the whole story—that makes all the pain and the waiting worth it. Jesus hasn't just come to bring healing but to destroy death itself.

This is why, over and over, even in the middle of the darkest, most hopeless-looking situations, Jesus says, *Don't be afraid.*

Not because life won't ever go wrong, but because nothing, no matter how bad—not even death—can separate us from his love and power. If we trust him, he'll take us *through* death into eternal life.

And one day in the future, when Jesus brings God's kingdom in all its fullness, he'll wipe out death, once and for all (Revelation 21 v 4).

The end of the story will make all the pain and the waiting worth it. Which means that, if we stick with Jesus, we have nothing in the whole world to be afraid of.

How might the hope that Jesus will one day put an end to death change the way you live today?

PRAYER

Loving Father, sometimes life just seems hard and cruel and painful for no reason. Often death feels sad and scary. In these times, please remind me of your unchanging love for me, and help me trust that one day you will make sense of everything. Amen.

✯ DAY 37 ✯
ORDINARY ✯

✯ **READ MARK 6 v 1-6**

Jesus returns home to Nazareth and, like last time, things don't go so well for him.

Entering the synagogue, Jesus sits down to preach. All around him are people who've watched him grow up. They know his family. They played with him as a kid. They were there as he learned to read, and dress himself, and help out with his dad's carpentry business. And now here he is, acting like he's some kind of big-shot prophet!

They're surprised. More than that, they're *offended*. Who does Jesus think he is? Does he honestly expect to fool *them*?

They're sure he's just an *ordinary* man, and so they're convinced that he has nothing to teach them (v 2-3). And because they won't hear Jesus out—because they won't come to him and ask—hardly any of them receive the help and healing that he's come to bring them (v 5-6).

It's true, though: on the outside, Jesus *does* look pretty ordinary (at least until he starts controlling the weather and raising the dead). He doesn't *look* like a warrior, or a king, or the Saviour of the world.

But through Jesus' ordinariness, something completely extraordinary is going on.

The real scandal is not *just* that this unknown carpenter from a tiny village in the middle of nowhere is actually a prophet, bringing good news from God (although Jesus is that). It's not even that he's God's promised Messiah (although he is that too).

The real scandal is that in Jesus, *God himself* has entered into the world he created.

The ordinariness of Jesus is not an accident or a mistake.

It's a sign of God's extraordinary love for us.

In Jesus, God has become fully human, because humans are exactly who he's come to save.

What would you expect God saving the world to look like? Would it be anything like this?

PRAYER

God, how huge is your love, that you would become part of your own creation to save and rescue us! Please help me understand more and more clearly what all this means for me. Amen.

⊒ DAY 38 ⊑

TRAVELLING LIGHT

READ MARK 6 v 6-13

What's your packing style when you're heading off on a trip? Do you travel light or pack absolutely everything you might need?

Jesus keeps travelling around, announcing God's kingdom—and now that he's spent some time showing his twelve disciples what that kingdom's all about, he sends them out to share what they've seen and heard.

But no one could ever accuse Jesus of being an over-packer. He specifically tells his disciples not to pack food, or a bag, or money, or even a change of clothes!

Why?

Jesus is teaching his friends that they can trust *him* to keep taking care of them, even when he's not standing right next to them anymore.

Sure enough, as the disciples head out, not only does Jesus make sure they've got what they need to survive, but he also helps them do incredible things they could never do on their own.

And the same is true for us. We can't see Jesus. And, short of a miracle, we *won't* see Jesus until the day when he returns to make the whole world new again.

But that doesn't mean he isn't with us.

Like the disciples, Jesus invites us to trust him, even while we can't see him. He has amazing plans for our lives. And as we put our trust in him, he'll help us put those plans into action.

That might not mean driving out demons or miraculously curing sick people. But it *will* mean being transformed more and more into who God made us to be as we turn to live his way (v 12). He will help us to love him and love others in ways we'd have no hope of doing on our own.

Do you think of Jesus more as a person from ancient history or the King of the universe? How can you remind yourself that he's both—and that he's right here with you today?

PRAYER

Heavenly Father, not being able to see you can make you seem so far away, but please keep teaching me what you taught your disciples: that wherever I am, you're with me every step of the way. Amen.

❯DAY 39❮

BETTER THAN GUESSING

READ MARK 6 v 14-16

As news about Jesus keeps spreading, people find all kinds of theories to explain what they're hearing.

Some say Jesus is Elijah, the great prophet from 900 years before (v 15).

Which isn't as random as it first sounds. See, according to Israel's Scriptures, Elijah had never technically *died*. Instead, God had sent a flaming chariot from heaven and taken him away in a whirlwind.

And if that wasn't strange enough, centuries later a prophet named Malachi announced God's promise to one day send Elijah *back* to his people, to prepare the way for God's coming.

So really, Elijah isn't such a bad guess (although, as Jesus will explain later, Malachi's "Elijah" promise was actually about John the Baptist, who was like a *new* Elijah, sent to prepare the way for Jesus' arrival).

Other people, meanwhile, think Jesus is a new prophet, bringing a new word from God (v 15—which is true, but not the whole story).

But King Herod makes the wildest guess of all: *Jesus is John the Baptist, back from the dead* (v 16).

Which, of course, makes *zero* sense.

And if Herod had actually investigated Jesus for himself—if he'd spoken to Jesus, or his family, or John's family, or the crowds who've seen John and Jesus hanging out together—he'd have known they were two different people.

But that's *not* what Herod does. Instead, he comes up with an opinion, and then just sits back and assumes he's right. As a result, he ends up further from the truth than anyone.

And this trap is just as easy for us to fall into today.

The world is full of opinions about God. But not every opinion is backed up by the evidence. And if God really has come here to earth, we can do better than just guessing about what he's like.

By investigating Jesus, we can figure out the truth.

What evidence do you have for your ideas about Jesus?

PRAYER

Loving God, please help me give less attention to people's loud, confident opinions about Jesus, and more attention to investigating Jesus for myself. Amen.

THE TRUE KING

After dropping the news that John the Baptist has been beheaded, Mark gives us a flashback to fill us in on what happened. John might have been all about God's kingdom, but that's not the only kingdom people have been talking about.

At this point in world history, the Roman Empire, ruled by Tiberius Caesar, stretches across Europe, northern Africa and the Middle East. It's so massive that Caesar needs a bunch of local rulers to help keep different regions under control.

Back when Jesus was born, Caesar's ruler in Israel was the murderous King Herod the Great, who killed anyone threatening his power, including his own wife and several of his sons. (And when Herod heard that toddler Jesus was destined to be King, he tried killing him too.)

Fast-forward 30 years. Herod the Great has died, his kingdom is divided between the sons he *didn't* kill, and now Herod Antipas is ruling in Israel's north. *That's* the Herod that John has been speaking out against: *The ruler of God's people should be following God's law, not stealing his brother's wife!* (v 18).

The wife Herod has stolen, Herodias, doesn't want to hear it. She wants John dead. But for now, Herod's protecting him. The crowds love John, and Herod knows they'll be furious if he kills him. But there's something else...

Herod's used to scaring people. But that doesn't seem to work on John. He's already told Herod things that others wouldn't dare to say. And even in prison, John keeps explaining how God wants Herod to live—and it seems like Herod can't quite shake off the truth of what John's saying. But Herod also knows that following John's advice will mean he can't keep living however he wants.

John says God's kingdom is greater than Caesar's or Herod's or anyone else's. And if God's the *true* King of Herod's life, that means Herod isn't. Sooner or later, Herod will need to decide whether he believes that.

How do you feel about the idea of God being in charge of your life?

PRAYER

Dear God, if you're the true ruler of my life... that means I'm not. Thank you that your amazing love and power mean this is actually great news for me. Amen.

★ ✦ DAY 41 ✦ ★
DECISION TIME

★ **READ MARK 6 v 21-29**

Have you ever done something you knew was wrong to avoid looking bad in front of your friends?

All along, Herod's been in two minds about John. John's message about God's kingdom is definitely *interesting*, but actually *joining* that kingdom would mean letting God change the way he lives.

Meanwhile, Herodias is still trying to get rid of John.

On Herod's birthday, the opportunity finally arrives—and it forces Herod to choose between God's kingdom and his own power and reputation.

Herod throws himself a party, invites the most powerful men in Galilee, and has Herodias's daughter brought in to entertain them. The men all watch her dance—and they like what they see.

Suddenly, Herod bursts out with an outrageous promise.

He'll give Herodias's daughter anything she wants! Up to half his kingdom!

Herodias seizes the opportunity. She sends her daughter back in to ask for John's head.

And now Herod has a choice to make. He can protect John or he can look strong in front of his dinner guests and protect his own reputation.

Herod makes his choice. He has John's head brought in on a platter. It's a horrifying scene, and it reveals what Herod *really* cares about.

God's kingdom was only ever *interesting* to Herod. He never let it change his life. And by having John killed, he got rid of the one person who was helping him understand who God was. The next time Herod appears in Jesus' story, he'll be mocking Jesus on the way to his death.

And though it might not happen in such a dramatic way, we all have the same choice to make about how we'll respond to the good news of God's kingdom.

Is Jesus just interesting to you? What do you think it might look like to let him actually start changing your life?

PRAYER

God, thank you that when you ask me to change, it's only ever to help me become more like Jesus. Please give me the courage to follow you, even when it means changing my life or risking my reputation. Amen.

◤ DAY 42 ◢ ✱

A NEW LEADER

✱ **READ MARK 6 v 30-34** ✱

After their time away announcing God's kingdom, the disciples gather back with Jesus, bursting with stories about the people they've healed and dark forces they've driven out through the power he gave them.

But one of the other biographies of Jesus tells us that their excitement is mixed with deep sadness too (Matthew 14 v 12-13). John the Baptist was a teacher to many of them, and a relative and friend of Jesus. His death hits them hard. Knowing they all need time to recover, Jesus takes them away to escape the crowds.

But the people see where they're headed and get there first. Some of them are still looking for a healing or a show—but more and more, the crowds are hoping for something else too. John's murder is just another reminder of what's wrong with Rome and the leaders they put in charge.

The crowds want a *new* leader. They want a Messiah to set them free.

Jesus has already been acting pretty Messiah-ish. And now he's brought his disciples to a remote place in the Galilean hills—which gets the crowds excited, because remote places in the hills are where rebellions get started.

In this same region, back when Jesus was a kid, a leader named Judas the Galilean gathered rebels to fight against Rome, stealing weapons and burning buildings. The Romans eventually killed Judas and ended his rebellion, but many in Israel hope a new leader will appear and succeed where Judas failed.

Jesus sees the crowds, lost and looking for a leader. His heart goes out to them. They're right to want change, and Jesus is the leader they've been waiting for.

But Jesus doesn't start handing out swords or whispering battle plans. He begins "teaching them many things" (v 34).

Because Jesus' answer to violence isn't more violence. It's the good news of God's kingdom.

How has Jesus already shown the power of God's kingdom in Mark's Gospel?

PRAYER

Dear God, in a world full of anger and violence, please show me how the good news of your kingdom has more power to change the world than any weapon. Amen.

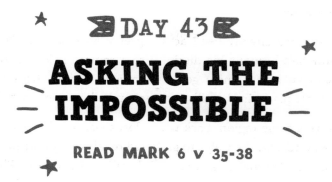

DAY 43

ASKING THE IMPOSSIBLE

READ MARK 6 v 35-38

Has someone ever asked you to do something completely impossible—something they should have *known* you had no way of doing?

At the end of a long day (which was *supposed* to be their day off), Jesus' disciples come to him with a request that sounds completely reasonable: *Send these people away to get something to eat* (v 36).

In response, Jesus asks them to do something that sounds completely *un*reasonable: "You give them something to eat" (v 37).

From what you know about Jesus, how hard would it be for him to sort this problem out himself? He could just say a word and cover the whole hillside in picnic baskets! But he doesn't. Instead, he deliberately involves his disciples.

And when they complain that they don't have enough, Jesus calmly asks them to bring what they do have—

which isn't much. But Jesus is about to turn it into more than enough for everyone.

Jesus knows his friends could never feed this crowd on their own. But they're not on their own.

And by asking *them* to feed everybody, Jesus is inviting his disciples to look past what they can do in their own power and to trust him to help them.

These events give us an important glimpse into what following Jesus looks like. Truly living the life that Jesus calls you to live is impossible to do on your own. Fully loving everyone around you is impossible to do on your own. Transforming into the person God made you to be is impossible to do on your own.

But you're not on your own.

Jesus invites all of us to look past what we can do in our own power, and to trust him to help us—because with Jesus, nothing is impossible.

Is there anything about following Jesus that seems impossible to you? What do you think Jesus would say about this?

PRAYER

Lord Jesus, thank you that when you ask me to do impossible things, you're always right there with me, ready to give me the help I need. Please help me with the things that feel too hard for me at the moment. Amen.

★ ⧫DAY 44⧫

BREAD FROM ★ HEAVEN ★

READ MARK 6 v 39-44

Centuries before Jesus arrived, God rescued his people from slavery in Egypt, and brought them through the wilderness to the new home he had promised them.

On the way, he fed them with bread, which appeared on the ground each morning. It was a daily sign of God's generous, dependable love; even in the middle of nowhere, he'd always provide for his people.

But God also reminded his people that they needed more than just bread to be happy and free. They needed God himself!

Years later, as Jesus hands out bread in the middle of nowhere, he's retelling that same story in a new way. He's reminding his people about what God is like.

God provides for his people. In God's kingdom, there is enough for everybody.

Whatever happens, Jesus' friends can trust him to give them everything they need.

And what they need most of all—even more than food!—is God himself. They need a way back home to God's kingdom. Which is exactly what Jesus has come to provide.

And as their response to his abundant generosity, Jesus invites his people to show that same generosity to others.

Generosity is hard because it always means giving up something that we could just keep for ourselves—our time, or our money, or our stuff, or our freedom to choose what *we* want instead of what's best for someone else.

But Jesus wants to turn his followers into people who are so sure we're going to be loved and cared for, no matter what, that we don't *need* to keep worrying about ourselves, because we know God will provide everything we need.

Instead, we can focus on loving him and loving the people around us.

How easy do you find it to be generous with your time, money and stuff? Is there anything in particular that God might want you to be more generous with?

PRAYER

Generous God, I'm sorry I find it hard to be generous. Please make me so convinced of your love and care for me that I can stop worrying about myself and focus on reflecting your generosity to everyone around me. Amen.

THREE IN ONE

READ MARK 6 v 45-46

Why did Jesus pray? However busy life got, Jesus always made time to get away and talk to God. Which might seem strange, given the hints we've been getting that Jesus *is* God. But Jesus isn't just talking to himself here.

God is absolutely unique in a bunch of ways, but possibly the most mind-bending is his *three-in-oneness*.

The Bible says there's only *one* true God of the universe, but that *one* God exists in *three* Persons: Father, Son and Spirit. We call this the Trinity.

Mark already gave us a glimpse of this, when Jesus was baptised: we saw the Father speaking from heaven to Jesus (the Son), while the Spirit hovered over him like a dove.

But the Father, Son and Spirit are not three *separate* gods, or three *thirds* of God, or three *forms* that God shifts between. They're *all* God, all together, all the time.

But they're also *distinct* from one another, and they have a *relationship* with one another.

Which is all brain-meltingly confusing, obviously.

But here's why it's also completely awesome and life-changing. Imagine God was just one and not *three-in-one*; before he made the universe, who was this God loving?

Well, nobody. There would've been nobody to love.

Love would be something this God *started* doing after he made the universe, and that he could just as easily *stop* doing one day in the future.

But God *isn't* just one. He's three-in-one.

And perfect love is something that's been going on *within* God—between Father, Son and Spirit—for all eternity. Love isn't just something God *does*. It's who God *is*.

When Jesus prays, he's continuing the perfect, loving relationship he's had with his Father since before the beginning of time. And as Jesus invites us into God's kingdom, he's inviting us to share in that exact same love.

How might this mind-blowing truth about God change how you see his love for you?

PRAYER

God, so much about you is hard to understand, but thank you for the simple truth of your perfect, unending love. Amen.

★ ⚔ DAY 46 ⚔
THE HEART ★

READ MARK 6 v 47-56

Have you ever heard someone say, "I *would* believe in God, if there was enough evidence," or "If I just saw a miracle for myself, *then* I'd believe"?

This kind of thinking seems pretty reasonable—but Mark's already shown us over and over again that it doesn't hold up to reality.

The Pharisees and teachers have seen Jesus perform incredible miracles—things no one but God could do. And still, they don't believe Jesus is who he says he is.

The problem isn't the evidence. It's how they've *responded* to the evidence.

And they're not the only ones with this problem.

By now, you might think nothing Jesus did could surprise his disciples. But as they see Jesus walking on the water, they're "terrified" and "completely amazed" (v 50, 51).

They still don't get who Jesus is.

Why? Well, it's clearly not a lack of evidence. Mark points us to the real issue: "Their hearts were hardened" (v 52).

When we think "heart", we usually think "feelings". "Following your heart" means doing what you *feel* you should do.

But the Bible uses the word "heart" very differently. The Bible's picture of our heart includes our feelings, but it also includes our *thinking*, and our *hoping*, and our *trusting*.

When the Bible talks about our heart, it's talking about what we love most in the whole world—what we're putting our ultimate hope and trust in.

And so whatever's going on in our heart is going to completely change how we act and how we respond to people.

Jesus' disciples don't need more information or evidence about Jesus. They've got plenty of that already. To really understand Jesus, they need to open their hearts to him— and the same is true for us.

What do you love most in the whole world? What are you putting your ultimate hope and trust in?

PRAYER

Father, please keep reminding me that you're not just a topic I can know *about*. You're a person I can get to *know*. Show me how to turn my heart towards you. Amen.

✴ ☒ DAY 47 ☒

CLEAN ON THE OUTSIDE ✴

READ MARK 7 v 1-7

Do you have any important family traditions? For the Pharisees, tradition was *everything*.

Another group of them arrive to check Jesus out—and, as usual, they don't like what they see. This time, they attack Jesus' disciples for eating without washing their hands properly.

In case we're wondering why they care, Mark provides some background (v 3-4). Remember all those add-on rules the Pharisees had come up with about how to *correctly* rest on the Sabbath—rules that weren't in God's law, but which they made everyone follow anyway?

Well, the Pharisees hadn't created add-on traditions just for the Sabbath. They had rules for *everything*. In this case, it's rules about washing.

The Pharisees aren't worried about germs here. These rules aren't about being *physically* clean on the outside.

They're about being symbolically, *ceremonially* clean on the inside.

The idea comes from God's law. God is holy and perfect, but we aren't. Our sin separates us from God, and so, before we can come home to God again, that sin needs to be dealt with.

While Israel waited for God's ultimate solution to this problem, he gave them symbols to act out—things they could do on the *outside* to remind themselves of their need to be healed and made clean on the *inside*.

Here's the thing, though: the only thing God's law said was that priests had to wash themselves before entering the temple to lead worship. But the Pharisees twisted that simple command into rules that said *everyone* had to wash, *every* day, before they ate.

And as they obsessed over following their own rules, they forgot that the rules were never meant to be the point.

Washing their hands couldn't fix their hearts. Following rules could never save them—and it can't save us either. Only God can save us.

What rules might you be tempted to follow as a way of trying to earn God's love?

PRAYER

God, keep reminding me that I can never earn your love. Help me trust in Jesus' goodness and not my own. Amen.

⚆ DAY 48 ⚆

DEVOTED TO GOD

READ MARK 7 v 8-13

Have you ever *said* you were doing something for one reason, when really you had a different, not-so-innocent reason for doing it?

That's what Jesus tells the Pharisees they're doing here. They might *say* they're all about following God, but they're actually way more concerned with keeping their own traditions (v 8). And not only are these human rules useless in bringing people closer to God; Jesus says they're actually pulling people in the *opposite* direction.

The heart of God's law is loving God and loving others—so the law was filled with rules explaining how to do that.

One big focus was honouring your parents. If you were an adult whose parents got into money trouble, it was your responsibility to help them. Back then, this sometimes meant selling an extra house or some land you owned and using the money to help your parents.

But the Pharisees had found a way around this responsibility.

To avoid giving up their property, they'd declare it "Corban"—*devoted to God.*

They still got to hold on to their property, but then when their parents came looking for help, the Pharisee could say, *Sorry, I can't sell this. It belongs to God now!*

God said, "Honour your father and mother" (v 10).

The Pharisees said, *I'm honouring God instead.*

But by ignoring God's call to help their parents, they weren't actually honouring God at all.

And as Jesus calls out the Pharisees for replacing God's rules with their own traditions, we should ask ourselves how we might fall into this trap.

We can't just make up our own ways of following God. *Actually* being devoted to God means paying attention to what he says is best.

When are you tempted to follow your own ideas about what's right and wrong instead of listening to God?

PRAYER

God, please help me notice situations where I might say I'm following you, but I'm actually just doing what I want. Help me to trust that your way is best and to be truly devoted to you. Amen.

⊰ DAY 49 ⊱

CLEAN ON THE INSIDE

READ MARK 7 v 14-23

After calling out the Pharisees, Jesus gathers the crowd together and shares his own teaching about cleanness and uncleanness.

He agrees with the Pharisees on the problem; our sin, our uncleanness, keeps us separated from God. But the Pharisees have missed the true source of that problem.

It's not what goes into your body that makes you unclean. It's what comes out (v 15).

The disciples ask Jesus to explain, and (even though he clearly thinks they should've worked it out themselves by now, v 18) Jesus breaks it down for them.

All the Pharisees' extra traditions miss the point. And even the good, original rules in God's law—about ceremonial washing or eating the right foods—can't actually *fix* the problem of people's sin. They're signs, pointing to something greater—reminders that what they really need is to be made clean on the inside, and that God's ultimate solution is still coming.

The real problem, Jesus says, is a heart problem.

All of our greed and lies and betrayal and unkindness, all the evil we do on the outside—it all starts on the *inside*, in our hearts.

We can make ourselves look as good as we like on the outside, but it's never going to fix what's really gone wrong between us and God.

And so the good news of God's kingdom isn't, *If you do everything right on the outside, God will love and accept you.* That was the Pharisees' game, and Jesus says it doesn't work!

The good news of God's kingdom is that *Jesus has come to make you clean and whole on the inside. He's come to give you a new heart.*

Where in your own life have you seen "evil thoughts" on the inside lead you into trouble on the outside? How does the good news of God's kingdom give you hope?

PRAYER

Loving Father, thank you that Jesus came to heal my heart problem and transform me from the inside out. Please keep changing my heart day by day, so I can truly be the person you created me to be. Amen.

⚔ DAY 50 ⚔
DOGS

READ MARK 7 v 24-30

Jesus leaves Israel and heads for Tyre. The people here don't worship the God of Israel, but news about Jesus has spread even here. A woman arrives, begging Jesus to drive out the spirit that's overtaken her daughter.

Jesus' response seems unusually cold: *First let the children eat. It's not right to feed their bread to the dogs* (v 27).

It sounds like an insult. But actually, it's a parable. And, as always when Jesus shares a parable, he's not shooing this woman away. He's inviting her into a conversation.

The key word in Jesus' parable is "first".

Jesus has come to help and heal the whole world, but he's come in a very specific way: as the Messiah that God promised to Israel.

Jesus has come to Israel *first*. But he's not here to help Israel instead of helping everyone else. By living out his role as Israel's Messiah, Jesus will make a way for everyone, everywhere, to come home to God: first Israel, and then the whole world.

But as Jesus showed by feeding the five thousand people, in God's kingdom there's plenty for everyone—and this woman knows it: *Okay, sure, you've come to Israel first. But isn't there plenty of God's love and grace to go around? Even the dogs get to eat the children's crumbs!*

She doesn't say she has a *right* to Jesus' help, or that she *deserves* it. Instead, she trusts in the love of God. And Jesus, seeing her faith, rescues her daughter.

Yesterday, we saw Jesus' own disciples being "so dull" about something Jesus said (v 18), and now here's this total outsider completely getting it!

God's kingdom is for everyone, everywhere—but you don't get in by deserving it.

You get in by recognising that you don't deserve it but trusting that Jesus loves you enough to bring you home anyway.

Do you feel like you deserve to be in God's kingdom? What about other people you know? How should we respond to the idea that there's lots of God's love and grace to go round?

PRAYER

Loving God, thank you that Jesus came to be not just Israel's Messiah but the hope of the whole world. Amen.

✹ ⚒ DAY 51 ⚒

MOGILALON ✶

READ MARK 7 v 31-37

Jesus leaves Tyre and moves through the Decapolis—the same Ten Cities which that guy from the tombs headed for after Jesus freed him from the legion of spirits.

Some people rush up, begging him to heal their friend. Mark uses a very particular word to describe the man—a word that gives us another big hint about who Jesus is.

The English words "could hardly talk" are a translation of the original Greek word, *mogilalon*—a word that's used only one other time in the whole Bible.

Centuries earlier, the prophet Isaiah had delivered a message to Israel: a time was coming when God himself would arrive to save his people.

"Then will the eyes of the blind be opened," Isaiah said, "and the ears of the deaf unstopped. Then will the lame leap like a deer, and the mute tongue shout for joy" (Isaiah 35 v 5-6).

When Isaiah was translated into Greek, that word "mute" was the same word: *mogilalon*—and this isn't just a coincidence. We're meant to connect these two parts of the Bible together.

Jesus leads the man away from the crowd—and even though he could easily heal him with just a word or a thought, he puts his fingers in the man's ears, touches his tongue, looks up to heaven and sighs deeply.

Why all the extra action?

Jesus knows this man can't hear—and so he speaks in a way he can *see*. As always, Jesus meets the person just as they are and gives them just what they need.

And as Jesus gives this *mogilalon* man back his speech and hearing, Mark invites us to look back through Israel's history and realise what this means.

Jesus is the one Isaiah talked about.

Jesus is God himself, arriving to save his people.

What do you think of the idea that Jesus meets us just where we're at? What do you think you need most from him?

PRAYER

Loving God, thank you for coming to save your world and its people, just as you promised. Help me to "shout for joy" at what you've done for me. Amen.

☰ DAY 52 ☱

SPOT THE DIFFERENCE

READ MARK 8 v 1-10

If you found yourself flipping back a few pages in your Bible to make sure you weren't re-reading an old bit by accident, that's totally understandable. Apart from some minor differences, this section of Mark's Gospel seems almost identical to one he recorded back in chapter 6.

So why tell us about this *second* almost-identical miracle?

Well, because it happened.

But then, there are plenty of things Jesus did that Mark doesn't record. As Jesus' disciple John once famously said, if every amazing thing Jesus did was written down, "even the whole world would not have room for the books that would be written" (John 21 v 25).

So why write down *this* event when it's so similar to one we've already seen?

Here's where we need to play Spot the Difference.

Last time, the crowd around Jesus had come from Galilee, which meant almost all of them were Israelites. But this time, Jesus is in the Decapolis, which means most of *this* crowd are probably outsiders to Israel.

Which makes three miracles in a row that Jesus has done in non-Israelite territory—which, if you were a bit put off by Jesus' dogs-under-the-table conversation before (7 v 28), should hopefully show that Jesus really does love and care for these people.

If the first feeding showed that Jesus wants to generously provide for everyone, this second feeding shows that "everyone" doesn't just mean Israel—it includes *anyone* from *anywhere* who puts their trust in Jesus.

But Mark's doing something else here too.

He's setting the scene for a conversation Jesus is about to have with his disciples—a conversation that will show how well they've been paying attention to everything Jesus has done and taught.

At this point in Mark's Gospel, how close do you think Jesus' disciples are to understanding Jesus' true identity? How close do you think you are?

PRAYER

Loving God, thank you that Jesus came for all kinds of people. Please help me to keep on seeing more and more clearly who he is, and what that means for me. Amen.

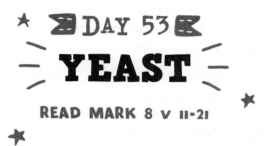

★ DAY 53 ★
YEAST

READ MARK 8 v 11-21

Jesus returns home and, again, the Pharisees attack: *Prove yourself. Prove you're not from God's enemy like we say you are.*

As if a sign from heaven would change their minds. As if he hasn't given them sign after sign already.

Jesus sighs deeply. He's not going to play their games. We've already seen that the Pharisees' problem isn't evidence. It's their hearts.

As Jesus and his disciples cross the lake again, he warns them not to let the same thing happen to them: *Beware the yeast of the Pharisees and Herod.*

Yeast is the ingredient that makes bread rise. A tiny bit of yeast spreads through a whole loaf of bread, transforming it completely. *Don't let the teachings of the Pharisees or Herod spread through your heart and mind, and transform you,* Jesus says.

The Pharisees and Herod don't care about God's kingdom. They just care about their own power and reputation. In fact, it's being focused on themselves that keeps them from seeing what the good news of God's kingdom is all about—enjoying living under God ruling as your King.

Don't be like them, Jesus warns.

But the disciples miss his point completely. They just think he's criticising them for forgetting to bring bread.

Jesus pulls them up: *Think about what you've just seen— twice now! Do you seriously think bread is a problem for me?* "Do you have eyes but fail to see, and ears but fail to hear?" (v 18).

But Jesus' questions aren't just some frustrated outburst. He's teaching them. Each question is guiding them one step closer to getting it.

As we saw two days ago, Jesus has come to help people who have ears but fail to hear. And as we'll see tomorrow, Jesus has come to help people who have eyes but fail to see.

Can you relate to the trouble that Jesus' disciples have in figuring Jesus out?

PRAYER

Dear God, when I read the Bible, I sometimes get the feeling there's something huge and important that you're trying to teach me, but I'm just not getting it. Please keep teaching and guiding me. Amen.

⚐ DAY 54 ⚐

LIKE TREES WALKING

READ MARK 8 v 22-26

Do you have eyes but fail to see? Jesus' question hangs in the air as he and his disciples meet an actual, real blind man.

Jesus leads him outside the village. And just as he spoke to the deaf man in a way he could see, Jesus speaks to this blind man in a way he can *feel*.

He spits on the man's eyes and puts his hands on him.

"Do you see anything?" (v 23).

"I see people; they look like trees walking around" (v 24).

It seems that something's gone wrong—like the miracle only half worked. But actually, Jesus has done this on purpose—because the blind man isn't the only one Jesus wants to help here.

This part's for his disciples.

It's as if Jesus is saying, *See this man? This is what you guys are like. You can see me—but the picture's still fuzzy.*

Don't worry, though. Watch what happens next.

Jesus reaches out to the man again. His eyes are opened. His sight is restored. He sees everything clearly.

Obviously, this is amazing news for the blind man. But it's amazing news for the disciples too; Jesus isn't going to leave them wandering around half-blind forever. He's going to stick with them until they see everything clearly.

And the same is true for anyone who puts their trust in him.

Paul, another one of Jesus' followers, would later put it like this: "For now we see only a reflection, as in a mirror; then [when Jesus returns] we shall see face to face. Now I know in part; then I shall know fully, even as I am fully known" (1 Corinthians 13 v 12).

Is this how you feel about following Jesus—that your picture of him is still fuzzy? What do you think Jesus would say about this?

PRAYER

Loving God, thank you that one day I will see you face to face and know you fully. In the meantime, please help me to keep seeing you more and more clearly each day. Amen.

⚑ DAY 55 ⚑ ★

WHO DO <u>YOU</u>
★ SAY I AM? ★

READ MARK 8 v 27-30

This is it. For months, Jesus' disciples have been digging into one all-important question: "Who is this man?"

And now we hit a turning point in Mark's Gospel, because here, at last, Jesus wants an answer.

He starts with an easier question: "Who do *people* say I am?" (v 27). The disciples recap the guesses we've heard so far. Some, like Herod, think he's John the Baptist. Some think he's the ancient prophet, Elijah, back from heaven to prepare the way for the Messiah's arrival. Some think he's another prophet.

Okay, great. But that was just a warm-up. Now Jesus comes to the *real* question: "But what about you? ... Who do *you* say I am?" (v 29).

Peter thinks it over. Jesus gives orders to storms, and they obey. He feeds huge crowds from almost nothing. He claims to forgive sins—which would be completely outrageous, except that then he backs up that claim by healing the sick and even raising the dead.

He talks constantly about God's kingdom, but he doesn't seem to just be *announcing* it, like John did. It's as if he's saying he's actually here to *bring* the kingdom.

Peter puts it all together. He figures out the answer: *You're the Messiah! The rescuing King God promised!*

Jesus immediately warns them not to tell anyone. Not yet.

For one thing, it would only end in violence. Violence from the crowds, who'd hear "Messiah" and think it was their cue to grab a sword and follow Jesus into an uprising against Rome. And violence from Rome and from King Herod, who'd quickly step in to crush that uprising.

This isn't what Jesus is about. Yes, he's God's promised, rescuing King—but his rescue will look like nothing anyone imagined. Meanwhile, the next words out of Jesus' mouth are about to turn the disciples' whole world upside down.

What about you? Who do you say Jesus is? And what difference does that make?

PRAYER

Lord Jesus, please help me, like Peter, to see that you're God's promised rescuing King—and to understand how this good news can transform my whole life. Amen.

⚰ DAY 56 ⚰
THE PLAN

READ MARK 8 v 31-33

Imagine you're Peter. You've watched Jesus' popularity skyrocket. You've seen his power. You've heard him speak out against the Pharisees and the imposter-king Herod.

And now he's just confirmed that he's the Messiah—God's promised King, and more powerful than Herod or even the emperor. He's been sent to free your people and rule the whole world!

What do you expect Jesus to say next?

Follow me to Jerusalem! Time to take my rightful place on the throne! Gather the armies! The tyranny of Rome ends here!

Whatever Peter expects, it's not this: *I have to suffer and be rejected and then die. But don't worry—I'll come back to life.*

Peter pulls Jesus aside. This is insane! The Messiah can't *die*! That's what *fake* messiahs do! That's how you know they're fake messiahs! Because they *die*, and everything they worked for falls apart! And now Jesus wants to do that *on purpose*?

He's meant to be their *rescuer*! How's he supposed to rescue anyone if he's dead? Jesus' plan is so completely *opposite* to Peter's expectations that he can't make any sense of it.

Meanwhile, Jesus hears in Peter's objections an echo of the whisper of Satan, God's enemy, tempting him away from what he *knows* God his Father wants him to do, just as Satan did back in the desert.

Jesus shuts Peter down. He won't be pulled off-course. Jesus hasn't made a mistake here. This is what God's been planning since before the beginning of the universe.

The problem isn't the plan. It's that Peter's perspective is too small. God is up to something way bigger and better and more incredible than the small-scale, limited human concerns filling Peter's mind. And he's inviting Peter (and us) to be part of it. But following Jesus will mean letting him completely mess with our expectations.

What expectations do you have about how your life should go? Have you got these expectations from Jesus or somewhere else?

PRAYER

Jesus, please keep expanding my perspective, so I can know you better and understand you more. Help me to follow you wherever it takes me. Amen.

THE UPSIDE- ★
DOWN PATH

READ MARK 8 v 34-37

Jesus has just announced his completely upside-down-sounding plan to give up his own life.

As if that wasn't shocking enough, now he tells the crowd, *If you want to follow me, this needs to be your plan too.* Following Jesus means *denying yourself.*

Which makes sense. If Jesus is the Messiah, the rightful King of the world—if he really is the one in charge—that means we're not.

Following Jesus means recognising that fact. It means our lives can't just be about grabbing onto our own rights and happiness anymore. They need to be about Jesus.

But Jesus isn't just standing back, ordering us around. He's inviting us to *follow him* along the path he's already on.

Jesus has *already* given up his own rights and happiness for us. And now he wants us to follow him—because making our lives about ourselves is a doomed plan anyway.

Jesus says that loving God and others is what we were made for. *That's* the true path to freedom. Living for anything else will only end up disappointing us.

Money, popularity, success or whatever else we might grab for ourselves might be fun for a while, but they'll all let us down in the end because we were made for something so much bigger.

Besides, none of that stuff lasts. Even if you gain the whole world, you'll eventually die and lose it all.

But Jesus has come to offer us life that lasts forever.

He's not inviting us to follow him *instead* of finding freedom and happiness. He's inviting us to follow him down this strange upside-down path, because it's *on this path* that true freedom and happiness are found.

Try to save our own life, and we'll lose it.

But if we give our life to Jesus, we'll find a life that's bigger and better than we ever dreamed.

Where are you looking to find freedom and happiness? Have those things ever let you down?

PRAYER

Lord Jesus, I'm sorry for when I've looked to other things to make me truly happy. Please keep helping me to see how following you is the only way to real freedom. Amen.

⊠ DAY 58 ⊠

LISTEN TO HIM!

READ MARK 8 v 38 - 9 v 8

Victory through dying. Resurrection from the dead. Losing yourself to find yourself. It all seems so impossible. So backwards.

But Jesus insists that this is how things really are. He *will* rise again after he dies. He'll live forever. And one day, he'll come "in his Father's glory with the holy angels" to heal and restore the whole world (8 v 38).

That day might be a long way off (two thousand years later, we're still waiting for it), but Jesus tells the crowd that they won't have to wait until then to "see that the kingdom of God has come with power" (9 v 1).

What does he mean?

For one thing, plenty of people sitting in this crowd will live to see Jesus' resurrection. But before that, three of Jesus' disciples are about to witness a mind-bending display of the power of God's kingdom.

Six days later, up on a mountain, Peter, James and John see Jesus completely transformed, shining with wondrous, terrifying glory. With *God's* glory.

He's joined by two towering figures from Israel's past: Moses, who'd led God's people out of slavery in Egypt centuries earlier and through whom God had given the law; and Elijah, God's great prophet. The point? All of the law, all the prophets, *everything* God's been doing, all through history—it's all been leading to Jesus.

The glory of God the Father comes down in a cloud, covering them all, and God announces that Jesus is his beloved Son—and commands what we should do in response: "Listen to him!" (v 26).

Jesus is God himself, here on earth as one of us. Listen to him because he's the King, and he deserves your attention. Listen to him because he knows what he's talking about. Listen to him because he loves you, and you can absolutely trust him.

How convinced are you that Jesus is worth listening to? As you keep reading Mark's Gospel, how can you tell whether you really are listening to Jesus or mainly ignoring him?

PRAYER

Loving Father, thank you for this extraordinary glimpse of Jesus' true identity. As I read Mark's Gospel, please help me to listen to Jesus and to respond with love and trust. Amen.

⚡DAY 59⚡

THE DAY OF THE LORD

READ MARK 9 v 9-13

As Peter, James and John leave the mountainside, heads swirling with everything they've seen, Jesus gives a familiar instruction: *Don't tell anyone.*

But this secrecy is only temporary. After Jesus rises from the dead, they can tell everyone (v 9).

The disciples discuss this. It must be another one of Jesus' parables, right? He *can't* mean he's *literally* going to die and rise again!

They know God's promise that, at the end of time, there'll be a great "Day of the Lord", when all his people will be raised to new life. But the idea that one *individual* dead person could just come back to life in the middle of everyday human history is unthinkable.

What can Jesus possibly mean?

Peter tries a different question: didn't God promise to

send Elijah again, before the Day of the Lord? And didn't they just *see* Elijah, up on the mountain?

What if that means that the Day of the Lord is coming any minute? What if there's no need for Jesus to die after all?

Jesus says that, yes, God *did* promise that "Elijah" would come. In fact, he's already come!

But that promise was actually about John the Baptist, God's *new* Elijah. And just as John suffered and died, now the Son of Man, Jesus himself, must also suffer and die (v 12).

Because, yes, God's prophets had promised that a Messiah was coming, who would rule forever. But they'd *also* promised that a suffering servant was coming, who would die to pay for the sin of the people.

And the shocking truth revealed by Jesus is that those two promised people are actually the *same person*.

Just as God promised, Jesus has come to rule forever. And just as God promised, Jesus has come to suffer and die.

How open are you to the idea of Jesus coming back to life from the dead? What do you think makes you feel that way?

PRAYER

Loving Father, thank you for sending prophets like Elijah to make such incredible promises to your people. Help me see how all those promises come together in Jesus. Amen.

⊠ DAY 60 ⊠ ★

UNBELIEVING GENERATION

★

★

READ MARK 9 v 14-19

Jesus, Peter, James and John find the other disciples surrounded by a crowd, locked in an argument. Jesus asks what's going on, and a man speaks up. He asked the disciples to drive out the spirit haunting his son, but they couldn't. Why?

Well, the teachers of the law might say that the disciples' failure proves that Jesus is a fraud or, worse, that he's on the same side as the evil spirit—but we know this isn't true (Mark 3 v 22-26).

The disciples might say that this particular spirit was too powerful or that Jesus hadn't given them the authority to deal with it. But this doesn't check out either (Mark 6 v 7).

Jesus hints at the real problem, calling them an *unbelieving generation* (9 v 19). Tomorrow, we'll see him explain what he means: they couldn't drive out the spirit because it could only be driven out through prayer (v 29).

Apparently, they've been trying to defeat the spirit *without praying*—without asking God for help. Instead of trusting in God's power, they've been trusting in their own. Unsurprisingly, it hasn't been enough.

The same is true for any follower of Jesus. Jesus invites you into a life that's impossible to live in your own strength. He might never ask you to drive out a spirit, but he'll ask you to love the people around you in other ways that feel just as impossible.

Generosity to people who don't deserve it.

Patience with the people who *most* frustrate you.

Repaying unkindness with kindness and evil with good.

If you try to live Jesus' way on your own, you'll just end up feeling burnt-out and frustrated because you don't have the power. But keep following Jesus, keep leaning on God's power, and he'll keep transforming you, a day at a time, into the person he made you to be.

What "impossible" acts of love might Jesus be calling you to today?

PRAYER

God, thank you that you're not limited by my limitations. I'm sorry for when I try to live your way in my own strength. Please help me to keep trusting in your power instead of mine. Amen.

The man's story of his son's suffering is brutal and heartbreaking: thrown into fire, half-drowned, driven mad by mysterious forces he can't control, over and over and over again, for years.

The father's desperation has brought him to breaking point. Already, Jesus' disciples have tried to help and failed. Maybe it really is hopeless. But he has to at least ask. *If there's anything you can do, please help.*

Jesus says that the question isn't *if* he can help. Of course he can. The question is, does the father believe it?

The man responds immediately, as if he's scared that Jesus might just walk away: "I do believe; help me overcome my unbelief!" (v 24). *Help me.*

And here, this poor, desperate father does what the disciples and teachers of the law have all failed to do; he admits his own helplessness and cries out to Jesus.

He's confused, and hurting, and his faith is still full of questions and doubts, but he brings all of that to Jesus. He brings what little faith he does have and asks Jesus for help—and he finds that that's all he ever had to do.

Jesus doesn't turn him away for not believing enough. He doesn't say, *Come back when you've stopped doubting.*

He drives the spirit out of his son, never to return.

Because it's not the *strength* of the father's faith that matters most. It's who he's putting that faith *in*.

Which is great news for us. Because, if we're honest, our faith is often a lot like this father's. We believe, but we wish we could believe more. Our faith is still full of questions and doubts.

But Jesus invites us to bring *all* of that to him—to bring what little faith we do have and to ask Jesus for help. And like the father, we'll find that that's all we've ever had to do.

Because it's not the *strength* of our faith that matters most.

It's who we're putting that faith *in*.

Are there any questions and doubts that you need to be honest with Jesus about? How does this story help you?

PRAYER

Lord Jesus, I do believe; please help me overcome my unbelief. Amen.

REAL GREATNESS

READ MARK 9 v 30-41 ★

What do you think makes a person truly great?

As Jesus heads home to Capernaum with his disciples, he explains again about the death he's heading for—this time with the added detail that he'll be "delivered into the hands" of the men who'll kill him (v 31). Jesus isn't just going to die. He's going to be betrayed.

The disciples still don't understand, and they're afraid to ask questions. Maybe they're scared that they won't like the answers.

All this suffering and dying talk doesn't fit at all with the kind of kingdom they want to see—one with an undefeated, unbetrayed and definitely un*killed* Jesus sitting on a throne, in a palace, ruling over the people.

And of course, once he's set up this kingdom, Jesus is sure to give positions of special honour and power to his *greatest* friends!

Which, funnily enough, they each seem to think means them.

Still, judging by the awkward silence when Jesus asks them about it, the disciples do seem to get that their argument is pretty embarrassing.

Jesus sits them down, and says they need to completely rethink their definition of greatness.

Chasing personal honour and power is *not* the way to greatness in God's kingdom. It's certainly not the path that Jesus himself is on. Jesus has come to serve and die—to put God and others before himself. *That's* the path to true greatness.

Then Jesus picks up a little child—the *least* great person in the room by their standards—and tells his disciples that loving and welcoming this kid would be the perfect place to start.

Because *really* welcoming God into their lives will mean loving and welcoming the people around them, especially people the world treats as unimpressive or unimportant.

Who in your life do other people treat as unimportant? How could you love and welcome them this week?

PRAYER

Dear God, thank you that there are no unimportant people in your kingdom but that you love and welcome everyone. Please teach me to do the same. Amen.

⚡DAY 63⚡
GEHENNA

READ MARK 9 v 38-50

What do you imagine when you hear the word "hell"? Underground caves? Red creatures with horns?

The disciples would have pictured something quite different—because the word "hell" that Jesus uses in verses 43-47 is a translation of the word "Gehenna", which was the name of an *actual place* outside Jerusalem.

Jerusalem was a city on a hill, surrounded by high walls, built to be a place of safety, security and community. Jerusalem was the king's city and, most importantly, it was home to the temple, where people could go to be with God.

Outside the city wall was Gehenna, the valley of Hinnom. Centuries earlier, in this valley, Israel's most wicked kings had burned their children alive as sacrifices to false gods. Since then, Gehenna had become a dumping ground for Jerusalem's garbage and sewage. Fires burned continuously to destroy the garbage, and the place was crawling with worms and maggots.

Inside the city was life, peace, joy and friendship with God. Outside the city was death, chaos, misery and separation from God.

And Jesus uses these images of life inside and outside *the city* to describe the difference between life inside and outside *God's kingdom*.

Jesus says the logical consequence of running away from God is ending up separated from him and his kingdom forever—which is like spending forever in the death, chaos and misery of Gehenna.

We'll think more about this passage tomorrow. But for now, know that Jesus doesn't tell us this just to freak us out but to show us what he's come to rescue us from.

We've *all* separated ourselves from God. Without Jesus, we're all on the road to "Gehenna".

But, through his death, Jesus has come to change all that and to welcome us home to God's kingdom—to an eternity of life, peace, joy and friendship with God.

What does it tell us about Jesus that he would willingly die to reunite us with God?

PRAYER

Lord Jesus, thanks for coming to welcome me home into God's kingdom. Help me to better understand what you died to save me from, so that I can see your love even more clearly. Amen.

⚔ DAY 64 ⚔

WHATEVER IT TAKES

READ MARK 9 v 42-50

Jesus uses some shocking language in this conversation. But if he really loves us, and if following him really is as infinitely, eternally important as he says, doesn't it make total sense for him to be this serious?

Jesus says that coming home to God is *so important* that you'd be better off diving into the sea with a giant stone around your neck than blocking or discouraging someone from getting to know Jesus (v 42).

It's *so important* that if there's anything hurting *your* relationship with Jesus—anything keeping you from loving and following him—it needs to go (v 43). Now.

If your hands lead you to do violence, cut them off!

If your feet carry you somewhere to do evil, cut them off!

If your eyes look out at the world with greed or jealousy, pluck them out!

Now, Jesus isn't *literally* telling us to mutilate ourselves. He's already said that it's our *heart's* rejection of God that separates us from him—not our hands or feet or eyes.

But this over-the-top language is meant to show us just how serious our situation is. Our sin separates us from God. Separation from God leads to death.

And even if we *did* remove our hands and feet and eyes, it still wouldn't fix our hearts. If we had to earn our way into God's kingdom by perfectly avoiding sin, we'd be doomed already.

Thankfully, being accepted into that kingdom doesn't depend on *our* perfection.

Jesus didn't come just to teach *us* how to be perfect. He came to be perfect *for* us.

Jesus has come to do whatever it takes to bring us back home to God.

He invites us to do, in response, whatever it takes to stay focused on him and the new life he died to bring us.

What habits or distractions are pulling you away from Jesus and the life he calls you to live? How can you get rid of them?

PRAYER

Loving God, please show me what's distracting me or leading me away from you, and please help me to cut it out. Amen.

⊠ DAY 65 ⊠
DIVORCE

READ MARK 10 v 1-12

The Pharisees attack Jesus with another question: *Is a man allowed to divorce his wife?*

Notice they don't bother asking if a *woman* can divorce her *husband*. In the ancient world, women rarely got a say. And when a man divorced his wife, he usually got to keep their house and money, often leaving her with nothing.

Some of Israel's teachers even said a man could divorce his wife if she accidentally burned his food or if he just found someone better-looking.

Do you agree? the Pharisees ask. *God did tell Moses in the law that a man could choose to divorce his wife.*

It's a trap.

If Jesus says divorce is *wrong*, isn't he contradicting God? (Not to mention contradicting Herod, who's already killed John the Baptist for criticising his divorce and remarriage.)

But if Jesus says divorce is *right*, isn't he agreeing that the Pharisees do understand the law after all? Shouldn't he follow all their other rules too?

Jesus doesn't fall for it. Instead, he goes for the heart: God created men and women to love one another as deeply and as faithfully as God loves us. He created marriage as a permanent commitment between a husband and wife that reflects his permanent commitment to us.

But God knows our hearts. He knows we mess this up. And so his law includes rules to *limit* divorce to when it's absolutely necessary and to *limit* the pain and injustice it can cause.

Divorce is a heartbreaking reality in our broken world. Sometimes marriages get so broken that divorce is the least bad option left. But this isn't how life is meant to be.

When God's kingdom comes in its fullness, we'll love each other perfectly. There'll be no more relationship breakdown. In the meantime, Jesus wants to teach us to love one another with more and more of the deep, faithful love he shows us.

Where have you seen examples of deep, faithful love?

PRAYER

God, thank you for loving us, even when we make messes of our relationships. Please help me to love others faithfully, just like you love us. Amen.

☰ DAY 66 ☰ ★

LIKE A LITTLE ★ CHILD ★

READ MARK 10 v 13-16

As Jesus teaches, people keep bringing their little children forward for him to bless.

The disciples have clearly forgotten what Jesus said before about welcoming little children in his name (9 v 37)—not to mention his *strong* warning against blocking or discouraging little ones from coming to know him (v 42)—because they try to shoo these kids and their parents away.

Jesus has important things to teach and people to heal! He doesn't have time to waste on blessing children!

When Jesus sees this, he's "indignant" (10 v 14). This is clearly a big deal to him.

Let the children come to me. Don't you dare keep them back! God's kingdom belongs to people like them. In fact, if you don't approach the kingdom like a little kid, you won't get in at all.

The disciples see these little children as just an annoying distraction, but Jesus says that *they* get God's kingdom better than anyone else here! Why?

Well, when it comes to God's kingdom, adults have all kinds of ways of missing the point. They try to impress Jesus with their greatness, like the disciples. Or they try to *earn* God's love with their goodness, like the Pharisees. And when they mess up, they worry that God won't love them at all.

Little kids, on the other hand, *know* there's plenty they can't do on their own. They know they need help—and they usually have no problem asking for it.

If we're going to enter God's kingdom, it won't be by earning or deserving it. Instead, Jesus says we need to come to him as a child comes to their loving parent: admitting our helplessness and receiving his blessing as a free gift.

How easy do you find it to trust that God's love really is a gift? When might you start acting like you can earn or deserve it?

PRAYER

Loving Father, thank you for this reminder that I can't impress you with my achievements or earn your love with my good behaviour. Please help me to stop trusting in myself and to receive your love as the free gift it really is. Amen.

⊠ DAY 67 ⊠

DEMOLISHING ∗ THE BARRIERS

★ **READ MARK 10 v 17-22**

A man falls at Jesus' feet: "What must I do to inherit eternal life?" (v 17). It's the question Jesus has just answered: *How can I enter the kingdom of God?* Except this guy apparently still thinks it's about being good, so he asks this "good teacher" what good thing he needs to do.

Jesus shows him his *real* problem. First, only God is truly good. (And sure, *we've* seen that Jesus is God himself, but this guy hasn't—so why's he calling Jesus good?) Second, if it's about trying to be good, hasn't God already described what "good" looks like in his law?

The man says he's *done* all that, but it still feels like something's missing. Jesus says there's just one thing: *Sell everything you own, and follow me.*

Hang on. What? Jesus hasn't asked anyone else to do this! Plus, hasn't he *just said* that you can't earn your way into the kingdom with good deeds?

Well, yes. But this isn't about earning anything. It's about demolishing this guy's barriers to following Jesus.

Remember when Jesus said, "If your hand causes you to stumble, cut it off" (9 v 43)? In other words, *Anything that's keeping you from fully loving and following Jesus needs to go.*

For this man, that means his *money* needs to go. Jesus knows this man loves his money more than he loves God—which means he *can't* follow Jesus until he gives it up, because following Jesus means putting God first.

The man's reaction proves Jesus right: his face falls. He goes away miserable. Given the choice between God and money, he picks money.

Jesus invites us to make a better choice—to trust that "treasure in heaven" (the eternal life and joy that comes with following Jesus) is better than any temporary treasure we might find here on earth.

What sort of things might be distracting you from fully following Jesus? Why is it sometimes hard to believe that what Jesus offers us is better?

PRAYER

Lord Jesus, please help me to see that your kingdom is worth more than anything I ever need to give up to get it. Give me the courage to get rid of anything that distracts me from following you. Amen.

✶ DAY 68 ✶
MONEY

READ MARK 10 V 23-31

You'd have better luck threading a camel through a needle than getting a rich person into God's kingdom (v 25).

But why? Why would riches keep you out of God's kingdom?

Well, first, being rich makes it dangerously easy for us to put our trust in *money* instead of God—to think we don't *need* God because, with enough money, we can solve our problems ourselves.

And second, we were created to love God and love people, but being rich makes it dangerously easy for us to fall in love with *money* instead.

Because, yes, having enough money to buy what we really need *is* a blessing from God—but we don't stop there, do we?

There's always something more to buy—always the next thing that makes us think, *I'd be happier if I had that.*

But the happiness never lasts. The new phone becomes the old phone. The new toy becomes the old toy. Which means we're *endlessly* chasing the next thing, and the next thing, and the next thing.

And so Jesus says that many people who look like they're coming *first* in life are actually coming *last*, because they're turning their backs on God to chase after endless *stuff*—and in the end they'll lose everything (v 31).

So who *can* be saved?

Nobody.

Well, nobody who's trying to do it on their own.

But in Jesus, God gave up all the riches of heaven to become a poor human, and to die for us, so that we could receive the *true* riches of eternal life with him.

The more that truth transforms our hearts, the less power money will have over us, because we'll know we've already got something way better than anything money can buy: friendship with God and eternal life.

How easy do you find it to be generous with your money? What does this say about the power money has over you?

PRAYER

Lord Jesus, thank you for becoming poor so that I could become truly rich. Please help me to put my trust in you and not in money. Amen.

THE CUP AND ★ THE RANSOM

READ MARK 10 v 32-45

Continuing towards Jerusalem, Jesus gives his most vivid warning yet of what's coming when they arrive.

Jesus will be betrayed and handed to Israel's leaders, who'll give him to the Romans, who'll mock him, spit on him, whip him and kill him.

And then he'll rise again.

But still, the disciples keep picturing Jesus on a throne, in a palace. And when that happens—when he's "in his glory" (v 37)—who'll sit at his right and left?

Sure, Jesus is Number One.

But who gets to be Number Two and Number Three?

When James and John volunteer themselves, Jesus starts talking about *drinking a cup*, a poetic image that God's prophets used hundreds of years before to describe receiving God's judgment for sin.

The other disciples crowd in, mad at James and John for swooping in to take the greatest positions in the kingdom—but again, Jesus explains that real greatness isn't about clawing your way to the top. It's about loving and serving others, even the people at the bottom.

That's why Jesus has come: to serve. To give up his life as a ransom.

Back then, if you owed someone a debt you couldn't repay, then instead of getting your money, that other person got you. You became a slave. And the only way out was if someone paid a ransom to buy your freedom.

Unless *someone else* paid the debt that you couldn't pay, you were trapped in slavery.

Jesus says that every one of us is trapped in slavery to our sin, which, in the end, means "drinking the cup" of death and separation from God's love.

But Jesus has come to drink that cup for us. He's come to give up his life, pay our ransom and set us free.

If this is what greatness looked like for Jesus, what do you think it should look like for us?

PRAYER

Loving God, thank you that, in Jesus, you've come to pay my ransom and free me from slavery. Please show me how to live as your ransomed child. Amen.

REAL FAITH ★

READ MARK 10 v 46-52

Jesus and his disciples reach Jericho, the last major stop on their way to Jerusalem. The streets are crammed with people flocking to Jerusalem for the Passover festival.

A voice cuts through the crowd: "Jesus, Son of David, have mercy on me!" (v 47). People try to shut him up, but he keeps shouting.

"Son of David" is another name for the "Messiah"—God's chosen King. Just as with the little children, it's the one everyone's trying to shush who most clearly gets who Jesus is.

Jesus invites Bartimaeus over. What happens next is like a beginner's guide to faith.

Bartimaeus has weighed the evidence about Jesus and decided that Jesus really is who he says he is. So he ditches the beggar's cloak he's been using to collect coins from passers-by. He leaves the *old* thing he was counting on to help him, trusting that Jesus is better.

Then, when Jesus asks what Bartimaeus wants him to do, he doesn't answer like James and John—he doesn't ask for greatness or power, and he certainly doesn't think he *deserves* Jesus' help. Remember, he was calling out for "mercy" (v 47, 48)—God's undeserved blessing. So when Bartimaeus comes face to face with Jesus, he admits his helplessness. He wants to see.

And, like everyone who asks Jesus for mercy, Bartimaeus gets it. In response, he leaves his old life behind and follows Jesus—and now his changed life is evidence to other people of Jesus' mercy and love.

This is what real faith looks like: being convinced by the evidence that Jesus really is the King. Leaving behind whatever else you've been counting on, trusting that Jesus is better. Admitting your helplessness, asking for God's mercy and getting it. And then following Jesus, and letting God use your transformed life to show other people the truth about himself.

If you haven't yet decided to follow Jesus, what do you think is holding you back? If you have, what's one thing you can do this week to point other people to him?

PRAYER

God, please help me to have faith like Bartimaeus. Use my transformed life to show others the truth about you. Amen.

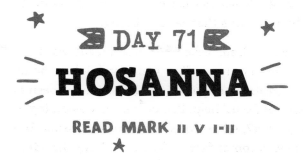

DAY 71
HOSANNA

READ MARK 11 V 1-11

When was the last time you were bursting with anticipation? You'd been waiting *forever* for something, and it was finally *almost time*!

That's the mood as the crowd approaches Jerusalem for Passover, the annual festival celebrating God's rescue of their ancestors from slavery in Egypt.

Except that now, for God's people living in Jesus' time, Passover brings mixed emotions. Because, yes, it's fantastic that God rescued his people back then. But what about now?

Sure, God's people are in their own land, but now it's a land under Roman rule. Roman soldiers walk their streets. Roman taxes empty their pockets. They're home, but they're not free. They long for God to do again what he's done before: to hear their cries and free them from their enemies.

And so now, as Jesus approaches Jerusalem, people get excited. They make a path of cloaks and palm branches, rolling out the red carpet to welcome King Jesus into his royal city.

Because surely *this* is what all the miracles have been pointing to! Surely Jesus has come to Jerusalem to set his people free! "Hosanna!" they shout. *Lord, come and save us!*

Again, they see what they want to see. None of them seem to notice the subtle message he's sending them.

He's not riding into Jerusalem on a mighty warhorse like a conquering king should. Instead, he's chosen a colt—a little donkey. It's as a signal to the crowd: *I'm your king. But I'm not who you think.*

Jesus *is* the Messiah they've been waiting for, riding into Jerusalem to set them free. But the Romans are only a temporary enemy—just the next in a long line of crooked human empires. Jesus has come to free them from their real enemy.

He's come to free them from sin and from death itself.

What are some ways in which you might be tempted to see Jesus as who you want him to be, and not as who he really is?

PRAYER

Lord Jesus, please help me not to be like the crowds, just seeing you the way I want to see you. Please keep showing me who you really are. Amen.

⬛ DAY 72 ⬛
TIME'S UP

READ MARK 11 V 12-19

I t's only April—a bit early for figs. But up ahead, Jesus sees a tree already covered in leaves, which means it should have figs too. As they get closer, though, there's no fruit to be found. And so Jesus condemns the tree: *Your time is up.*

What's going on here? As Jesus heads for the temple, we'll find some clues.

Worshipping God at the temple involved sacrificing animals as a way of paying for your sins (not that these sacrifices could *actually* heal anyone's relationship with God; they were symbols, pointing ahead to God's ultimate answer).

The temple priests have turned these sacrifices into big business, setting up stalls in the temple courts which sell animals at over-the-top prices. Others charge big fees to swap money from one currency to another. It's totally unjust and unfair. They're taking advantage of people who are coming to worship God.

God's house of prayer has become "a den of robbers" (v 17). Jesus is furious. But when he starts flipping tables, he's not losing his temper. He's making a very deliberate statement: God's people have become like the fig tree.

A tree with big, green leaves like that *should* be producing fruit. The fact that it wasn't showed that the plant was diseased or dying inside. If there wasn't fruit by now, there never would be.

In the same way, Israel's leaders *should* be guiding people to God, but their mistreatment of the temple shows that something's gone deeply wrong inside their hearts— something they can't fix by themselves.

Jesus' verdict on the fig tree is a picture of his verdict on Israel's leaders: *Your time is up.*

Thankfully, the temple and its sacrifices weren't God's ultimate answer to the problem of our sin. They'd been a preview of the ultimate way in which God would come to help his people—the ultimate place where they could come to have their sins forgiven.

Now, in Jesus himself, that answer has finally arrived.

How do you feel about the idea of Jesus getting angry at injustice?

PRAYER

God, thank you that, in Jesus, you have made a way to heal our relationship and bring me home to you. Amen.

☒ DAY 73 ☒

VENDING MACHINE

READ MARK 11 v 20-25

Imagine putting money into a vending machine, only to watch your chocolate bar get stuck behind the glass. It'd make sense to ask what's *wrong* with the machine. You told it what you wanted, but it didn't deliver!

But now imagine that you ask your friend for a chocolate bar and they say no. Hopefully your reaction wouldn't be, "What's *wrong* with you?"

Because your friend is not a vending machine. They could have all kinds of excellent reasons for not giving you the chocolate.

Your friend is a person. You need to treat them like one.

In today's reading, Jesus teaches his disciples about prayer. When they're amazed by the withered fig tree, Jesus says that if they have faith in God, *anything* is possible—even uprooting a mountain!

God *can* do anything we ask. And at first, it looks like Jesus is saying he will do *anything* we ask, if we just believe hard enough.

But God isn't a vending machine. It's not like we just put in our prayers and get out a chocolate bar (or whatever else we want). Having faith in God means trusting that his way is best. He might have all kinds of excellent reasons for not answering our prayers in the way we expect.

Jesus also connects prayer to forgiveness; part of trusting that God's way is best is being as absolutely committed to forgiving other people as he is to forgiving us.

If you treat God like a vending machine, you'll quickly be disappointed. But the more you see prayer for what it really is—an amazing opportunity to personally connect with the God of the universe and to get on board with what he's doing in the world—the more life-giving and worthwhile you'll find it.

When might you be tempted to treat God like a vending machine? What might it look like to treat him more like the God he is?

PRAYER

Loving God, thank you that you're a real person I can really get to know. As I keep figuring prayer out, please keep reminding me that you love me and that I can trust you. Amen.

TROUBLE COMING

★ READ MARK 11 v 27-33 ★

You know that feeling when you're watching a scary movie and the tension suddenly ramps *way* up? Everything slows. The music turns menacing. You twist in your seat, knowing that any minute now there's *major* trouble coming.

That's what it's like as Jesus returns to the temple. Many in the crowd are *itching* to rebel against the Romans, and they want Jesus to lead them. He could just say the word, and the blood will start flowing.

The Romans *know* Israel hates them. And if trouble starts, they know it'll start here in the temple, at Passover. But they're ready. A massive army barracks—the Antonia Fortress—looms overhead, packed with soldiers ready to rush out and fight violence with violence.

Meanwhile, Israel's leaders still want Jesus dead. But if they just *grab* him, they'll anger the crowd, which could bring the soldiers running.

Instead, they try to trap him into turning the crowds against himself. *Who gave you the right to bring trouble into our temple?* they ask.

Clearly *they* never gave him that authority. So was it God—or just Jesus himself?

If Jesus says *God*, they'll say he's making it up. They'll accuse him of being a false prophet, which is punishable by death. But if Jesus says *himself*, isn't he admitting that he doesn't have any real authority at all?

Seeing the trap, Jesus turns the question back on them: *Who gave John the Baptist the right to do what he did? Because my authority is from the same place.*

And now it's the leaders who are cornered. If they say *God*, they're admitting that they should've believed John—and that they should believe Jesus too. If they say *people*, then the crowds—who *did* believe John—will be furious.

Instead, the leaders say they "don't know" the truth (v 33). But is that *really* the case? Or are they really just *avoiding* the truth because they don't want to hear it?

Is there anything Mark has written that you would prefer wasn't true? Why?

PRAYER

Dear God, please give me the courage to honestly seek the truth, trusting that you'll help me find it. Amen.

✦ DAY 75 ✦

✦ THE CORNERSTONE

READ MARK 12 v 1-12 ★

Having silenced the religious leaders, Jesus shares a parable that they quickly realise is all about *them*.

Like the vineyard-owner finding tenants to care for his vineyard and help its grapes grow, God found priests and leaders to care for Israel and help its people grow closer to him.

And like the vineyard-owner sending servants to visit his tenants, God sent prophets to his people, all the way up to John the Baptist. But just as the tenants beat up and killed those servants, so Israel ignored and mistreated God's prophets.

Finally, the vineyard-owner in Jesus' parable sends his own son: the one destined to own this whole vineyard. Surely the tenants will respect *him*!

Instead, they murder him and throw away the body.

And this, Jesus says, *is exactly how you're treating me.*

But just as with the tenants in the parable, things won't go the way Israel's leaders want. By fighting Jesus, they're fighting God himself. And thanks to their shameful treatment of God and his Son, they're hurtling towards their own doom.

Jesus ends the parable by describing himself with a quote from Israel's Scriptures—the writings these guys are meant to be experts on.

Jesus is like a stone that gets rejected by the builders but then ends up becoming the cornerstone—the stone that holds the whole building together!

Israel's leaders have rejected Jesus. Even now, they're plotting to kill him. But that won't for one second put the brakes on God's rescue plan.

In fact, as he's been telling his disciples for months, it's exactly *by* being rejected and killed that Jesus will carry that rescue plan out.

It seems like almost everyone who actually met Jesus either wanted to kill him or worship him or crown him king. Why do you think Jesus provoked such extreme reactions?

PRAYER

Lord God, you worked even the schemes of Jesus' worst enemies into your plan to save us. Thank you that nothing on earth can derail your good plans for us. Amen.

WHOSE IMAGE?

READ MARK 12 v 13-17 ★

Israel's leaders are still hoping to arrest Jesus, so they send another crew to trap him with another question: *Should we pay Caesar's poll-tax?*

Besides their regular taxes, the Romans made the people they'd conquered pay an annual tax of one silver denarius to Caesar, just for living in the empire. Caesar made Israel *pay* to be ruled by the empire they hated!

Remember Judas the Galilean, who led the violent rebellion against Rome, back when Jesus was a kid? It was *this tax* that made Judas mad enough to start that rebellion.

And now here's Jesus, also from Galilee, bursting into the temple, talking about a kingdom that's greater than Rome.

If Jesus says, *Don't pay Caesar's tax*, it'll sound like he's calling for another rebellion, and the Romans might just do to Jesus what they did to Judas.

But if Jesus says they *should* pay the tax, the crowds will turn on him, because how can Jesus be serious about God's kingdom if he's bowing to *Caesar's* kingdom?

"Bring me a denarius," Jesus says. "Whose image is this?" (v 15-16).

Well, it's Caesar's face on the coin. He's minted this money with his image on it, to bring himself glory and show the world what he's like.

But, as everyone listening knows, Caesar isn't the only one who's put something out into the world with his image on it.

When God created human beings, he made us in *his* image (Genesis 1 v 27), to bring him glory and to show the world what he's like.

And so Jesus says, *Sure, give Caesar back what belongs to him—but remember that you don't belong to him. Whatever Rome says, you all know who the real King is. Make sure you give him what he deserves too. Give Caesar his little coin. But give your true commitment to God.*

Are you treating God as your real King, or is something else getting your highest commitment?

PRAYER

God, please help me to live wisely in your world, never forgetting who my true King is. Amen.

⚊ DAY 77 ⚊
GOD OF THE
✦ LIVING ✦

READ MARK 12 v 18-27

Can we *really* believe in resurrection—in people coming back to life again after they die?

The Sadducees, another group of Israel's leaders, say *no*— and they invent a story to show that the whole idea is ridiculous.

It's a *weird* story though, right? Why on earth are seven brothers all marrying one woman?

Well, according to God's law, if a husband died before his wife had children to look after her, his brother *had* to marry her. Remember, in the ancient world, women who suddenly found themselves with no husband or children often wound up with nothing. This marry-the-brother law was meant to make sure women in these tragic situations were looked after.

But the Sadducees' story takes this idea to the extreme: *Let's say it happened not just once but seven times. If all seven men are coming back to life one day, won't this woman end up with seven husbands?*

It's ridiculous! And it's meant to make *Jesus* look ridiculous.

But since they mentioned Moses, Jesus uses Moses to show their mistake; Abraham, Isaac and Jacob had already been dead for centuries by the time God spoke to Moses.

But God didn't tell Moses, *I was their God.* He said, *I am their God.* God knows Abraham, Isaac and Jacob aren't gone forever. He's still their God. And because they belong to him, they'll return at the resurrection.

If the Sadducees understood the *Scriptures*, they'd get that (v 24). And if they understood the *power of God*, they'd know that on that great resurrection day, *everyone* who belongs to God will be raised to new life (1 Thessalonians 4 v 13-18). And then we won't even *need* marriage anymore (Mark 12 v 25), because even the best marriage is just a shadow of the unimaginably greater love and joy that will be shared by God and his people forever.

Do you think God's promises about the future sound like good news? Why?

PRAYER

Loving God, thanks for your promise that everyone who belongs to you will be raised to new life with you when Jesus returns. Thank you that by trusting in Jesus, I can be included in that promise too. Amen.

⧸DAY 78⧹
LOVE

READ MARK 12 v 28-34

Of all the commandments in God's law, which is the most important?

To answer, Jesus quotes some words that God spoke to Israel centuries earlier, which have become a daily prayer for his people—words that remind Israel that they belong to the one true God and should love him with everything they've got.

This, Jesus says, is the greatest commandment.

But why would God *command* people to love him?

Well, it's true that God *deserves* our love. He created the universe and gave us life!

But God doesn't *need* our love. He's not lonely or empty or desperate for friends. The three-in-one God of the universe is already *overflowing* with love. He made us to share in this endless love he already had.

And through his love, God shows us what real love looks like: choosing to put others first and work for their well-being, no matter how they treat you.

Our love for God is only ever a *response* to his love for us.

And because God's love is what we were *created* for, when God calls us to love him, he's calling us onto the path of our truest freedom and joy.

And this means we need to love other people too—because loving people is a huge part of how we show our love for God.

At least, that's how it's *supposed* to work.

But none of us actually live like this. We don't love God or each other the way we should. And as a result, we separate ourselves from God's love.

Which leaves us lost and in need of a rescue.

Jesus has come to carry out that rescue. But bringing us home to God will take the greatest act of love the world has ever known.

Why do you think we find love so hard?

PRAYER

God, I'm sorry that I don't love you or other people as fully as I should. Thank you for coming as Jesus to live the perfect life of love that I couldn't live and to give that life up for me. Please help me to love like you. Amen.

⊠ DAY 79 ⊠
SON OF DAVID

READ MARK 12 v 35-37

A thousand years before Jesus was born, when Israel was still a free nation, it was ruled by King David—a man hand-picked by God himself. David wasn't perfect, but he was still the greatest king in Israel's history.

But God promised that one day, an even greater king would be born into David's family: the Messiah.

And since the Messiah would be a son of David, most people in Jesus' day assume he will do what David did: gather armies, overthrow Israel's enemies, and bring peace and freedom to their country.

The thing is, though, Jesus says, *if the Messiah's one of David's descendants, why would David ever refer to him as "Lord"?*

"Lord" was a title you'd use for someone more honoured and important than yourself—and back then, the father was always more honoured than his sons.

A man in David's culture would *never* call his son or grandson "Lord". That's what his sons and grandsons would call *him*!

So how can the Scriptures say that the Messiah is David's son *and* David's Lord?

Well, there is one person in Israel who's more honoured and important than Israel's king—and that's Israel's *God*.

Which means that Jesus' question to the crowd is hinting at an absolutely explosive truth: Jesus, the promised Messiah, *is* David's son—a human being, born into David's family.

But he's also David's *Lord*. Jesus is God himself, here on earth to save his people.

And just as Jesus' *identity* is way bigger than anyone saw coming, his mission is way bigger too. He's not just here to bring peace and freedom to Israel. He's here to bring it to the whole world—not by overthrowing the Romans but by overthrowing death itself.

What's your reaction to Jesus' not-so-subtle hint that he's God himself? What would it look like to treat him as your Lord?

PRAYER

Lord, thank you that your plans for your people are always bigger and better than we can see coming. Help me to keep on being amazed by everything you've done for me. Amen.

⊠ DAY 80 ⊠

A PICTURE OF GREATNESS

READ MARK 12 v 38-44

If the teachers of the law hadn't already been plotting to kill Jesus, hearing him call them out in public like this would definitely have done the trick.

Jesus does not hold back. He says they're dangerous, self-obsessed frauds. They should be showing Israel how to live God's way, but instead, they just want to show everyone what a big deal they are.

They *love* being invited to the best parties and getting the best seats. They parade through town in fancy clothes, just so people will bow and wave and make them feel important. They pray big, long, loud public prayers—not to actually connect with God but just to impress everyone who's listening.

They put on a big show of obeying God's law, but they ignore the *heart* of God's law. Instead of looking after vulnerable women who've lost their husbands, they cheat them out of whatever houses or money they might have left.

And speaking of vulnerable widows...

Jesus goes in to watch the place where people donate money to the temple. The big donations don't impress him. But when a widow drops in two tiny coins, he points her out to his disciples—because this whole scene is a picture of what the upside-down greatness of God's kingdom looks like.

The teachers *look* all great and impressive, but their hearts are far from God, and if they don't return to him, they'll end up losing everything.

The widow looks completely *unimpressive*, but unlike the rich people who just toss God their extra money, she loves and trusts God with *everything she has*. And because she's putting her hope in him, she'll end up gaining the *infinite* riches of eternal life in his kingdom.

What do you think your actions on the outside show about who you really are on the inside?

PRAYER

Loving God, I'm sorry for when I'm only concerned with looking good. Please change me on the inside, and let that shine through on the outside too. Help me to show the same love and generosity to others that you've shown to me. Amen.

STAND FIRM ★

★ READ MARK 13 v 1-13

Jesus' disciples are blown away by the temple; it's so enormous and incredible! The temple and its courts take up a quarter of the whole city, and some of its stones weigh *hundreds* of tons!

Yes, says Jesus, *and soon it'll all be destroyed* (v 2).

It's a shocking announcement. And later, as the disciples gaze down at the temple from the Mount of Olives, they ask, "When will these things happen?" (v 4).

(Remember the phrase "these things". We'll need it later.)

Jesus answers their question—but at the same time, he also zooms way out to talk about the bigger picture. He describes not just the *temple's* future but the future of the whole universe.

All along, Jesus hasn't *just* been preparing his disciples for his death and resurrection. He's been preparing them for what comes next. After Jesus dies and rises, he's going back to heaven. Then, sometime in the future, he'll return to earth, bringing God's kingdom in all its fullness.

But while they wait for Jesus' return, it'll be his followers' job to spread the good news of Jesus to the whole world, so others can join God's kingdom too.

And Jesus warns them that during that time, there'll be *all kinds* of drama. This does include the destruction of the temple, but it includes way more than that.

There'll be false messiahs, broken families, war, betrayal and natural disasters. And Jesus' followers will be hated and mistreated for following him.

Which all sounds terrible. But Jesus' command to his followers (both back then and today) is stand firm and *don't worry* (v 13, 11).

Because whatever happens before Jesus returns, God will be with his people, through his Holy Spirit, every step of the way—and everyone who stands firm in him will be saved.

Have you ever been mistreated for following Jesus, or do you know someone who has?

PRAYER

Lord Jesus, please help me to stand firm, trusting you, no matter what. When I'm tempted to worry, remind me that whatever happens, my future is safe with you. Amen.

DON'T WORRY

★ **READ MARK 13 v 14-27**

Do you ever feel crushed by all the evil and chaos we see in the world? It can feel so overwhelming—like the whole world is ending.

Turns out that's not a new feeling.

In 66 AD, Israel's anger at Rome boiled over into all-out war. The people finally got their violent rebellion—with devastating results.

In 70 AD, the Roman general Titus demolished Jerusalem's walls, destroyed the temple, and burned Jerusalem to the ground. In the place where Israel had worshipped God, Titus made sacrifices to the false gods of Rome. It was an *abomination*—a disgusting and shameful act.

As he teaches his disciples, Jesus knows all this is coming. He knows the prophet Daniel's vision of an "abomination that causes desolation" is about to come true (v 14).

And, Jesus tells his followers, *when it happens, get out of there*—because when Jerusalem falls and the temple is destroyed, it's going to feel like the end of the world.

But it won't be. As tragic as the city's destruction will be, history will continue.

From the very beginning, nations and empires have risen and fallen. People have done endless violence and evil to one another. This was true before Jerusalem fell, and it'll be true after.

And so Jesus' warning to his disciples is *also* a warning for us today: we should *expect* more war and chaos. More abominations. More impressive-sounding voices trying to lead us away from Jesus.

But the call of Jesus remains the same: *stand firm* and *don't worry* because things won't be this way forever.

One day, Jesus will return to gather all his people to himself (v 26-27). And when he does, there is no evil or chaos in all creation that Jesus won't put right.

How should this comfort us when we see death and destruction on the news or in our own lives?

PRAYER

Lord God, when I feel overwhelmed by the world's evil, remind me that the forces of darkness cannot and will not win. Help me trust you in the chaos. Amen.

KEEP WATCH

READ MARK 13 v 28-37 ★

All through this conversation, Jesus has been doing two things at once.

He's been answering his disciples' original question: *When will the temple be destroyed?* But he's also been zooming out from this one event and using it to talk about where *all of history* is heading—which means talking about the day when he'll return.

The disciples might assume both events will happen at the same time, but that's not what Jesus is saying.

When Jesus says, "This generation will certainly not pass away before all these things have happened" (v 30), he's talking about the same "these things" the disciples first asked about: the destruction of the temple and the fall of Jerusalem.

And he's right. Within forty years of their conversation, Jerusalem will be a pile of rubble.

As for Jesus returning to gather his people and set up God's kingdom here on earth... that's a whole different timeline. Jesus says not even *he* knows the day or hour that will happen; only God his Father does (v 32).

But one thing's certain: Jesus' words will never pass away. Everything he's promised will happen (v 31).

And so, on top of *Stand firm* and *Don't worry*, Jesus adds a third command: *Keep watch* (v 33).

Because Jesus could be back *any time now*, and if we're not ready and excited about that, something is seriously wrong.

When Jesus returns, God's kingdom will fill the earth, driving out all evil, everywhere—and he invites us to be a part of that (v 34)! Following Jesus means that our future is *absolutely secure*. His return means that the cycle of human violence and destruction will finally be broken, once and for all.

How could we not hope and watch for it every single day?

How should trusting Jesus' words change how we live, here and now? What hope do Jesus' promises hold for the billions of people around the world experiencing deep pain and suffering?

PRAYER

Loving God, please show me that your promises are true—and let that truth transform my life from the inside out. Help me to keep watch and look forward to Jesus' return. Amen.

⚔ DAY 84 ⚔

EVERYTHING ★ SHE HAS

READ MARK 14 v 1-9

By now, Israel's leaders have given up on trapping Jesus in his words or turning the crowds against him. They've come up with a new plan, and it's a whole lot simpler: they'll just kidnap Jesus and kill him.

But they can't grab him in public, during the festival, or the crowds will riot. If this plan's going to work, it'll have to happen in secret.

Jesus, meanwhile, is just outside the city in Bethany, visiting "Simon the Leper" (v 3)—although clearly this guy doesn't have leprosy anymore, or he wouldn't be allowed home. This is probably someone Jesus has healed: maybe even that leper we met way back in Mark 1.

Anyway, sometime during the meal, a woman approaches Jesus with a jar of perfume. Which isn't so unusual. Back then, to honour and welcome an important guest, you might sprinkle a few drops of perfume over their head.

Only that's not what this woman does.

Instead, she breaks open the perfume—a jar that someone would've worked for a *long* time to afford—and pours the whole lot out over Jesus.

The other guests call it a waste, but Jesus says they're missing the point. Of *course* helping the poor is incredibly important—but this is an extravagant, extraordinary act of love, and it deserves to be celebrated.

Like the widow in the temple with her two coins, this woman pours out everything she has. She does what she can to love and serve Jesus, and that's absolutely never a waste.

But there's more, because there's another time you might pour perfume over someone: when you're preparing their body for burial. Whether she knows it or not, Jesus says *that's* what she's done for him.

And 2,000 years later, her selfless love is still being celebrated.

How could you follow the example of these two generous women?

PRAYER

Loving God, you have been so extravagantly generous to me. Help me to remember this and to be extravagant in the way that I live for Jesus. Amen.

✠ DAY 85 ✠ ★

BETRAYED

★
READ MARK 14 v 10-21
★

Israel's leaders are stuck. During the day, they can't arrest Jesus because of the crowds. But at night, they can't *find* Jesus—because Jerusalem's so packed that he can just slip away.

Then suddenly, the solution falls right into their laps. It's the betrayal that Jesus knew was coming (10 v 33). Judas, one of his own disciples, has turned against him.

Maybe Judas never bought that Jesus was the Messiah. Maybe he checked out when he realised that following Jesus wouldn't mean power and riches.

Whatever the reason, Judas doesn't just quit and go home. He heads straight to the chief priests to sell Jesus out.

From then on, Judas watches for his chance. When the disciples ask Jesus where they'll be sharing the Passover meal, picture Judas leaning in, waiting for an address to tell the chief priests.

But Jesus doesn't give him one. Instead, he gives some weird instructions about following a guy with a water jar—instructions that will guide his disciples to the place but that'll be completely useless for the priests to try to follow later.

Over dinner, Jesus tells his disciples that there's a traitor in the room—but interestingly, he doesn't say who. Maybe Jesus wants to give them *all* the chance to think about where they stand with him.

They all swear it's not them, but Jesus insists: he *will* be betrayed—but even *this* is part of God's plan (14 v 21).

Judas might think he has it made, but he's just sealing his own destruction.

Meanwhile, what Judas means for evil, God will turn around and use for good. Jesus' death can't possibly derail God's plan—because Jesus' death *is* God's plan.

Have you been betrayed by someone close to you? How does it feel to know Jesus understands first-hand what that's like?

PRAYER

Jesus, it's hard to think of a worse feeling than being betrayed by a friend—but this was just the *start* of the pain you went through for me. Help me to see all this for what it is: proof of your extraordinary love. Amen.

⚡ DAY 86 ⚡
PASSOVER

READ MARK 14 v 22-26

The Passover meal has a *long* history. It began with the last meal that God's people ate before being freed from slavery in Egypt.

Leading up to that night, God had given Pharaoh, Egypt's king, warning after warning to free his people. He'd done incredible miracles to show that this was a fight Pharaoh couldn't win.

But still, Pharaoh refused to let Israel go—until God delivered his last, worst warning; to finally end Pharaoh's evil, God's judgment was going to sweep through Egypt, and the eldest son in every family would die.

But for anyone who trusted him, God offered a way out.

He told each family to sacrifice a lamb, eat it and paint the doorframe of their house with its blood. Everyone who did this would be safe. God's judgment would *pass over* them. They would live, because the lamb had died in their place.

By trusting in the sacrifice that God had provided, his people were saved.

That very night, they walked free from slavery.

As Jesus and his disciples celebrate the Passover, they're remembering that incredible rescue, centuries before. But this Passover, God is launching an even greater rescue.

To explain, Jesus takes bread, breaks it apart and hands it to his disciples.

My body is like this bread. It will be broken apart for you.

He takes a cup of wine and passes it around to his disciples.

My blood is like this wine. It will be poured out for you.

Again, God has come to rescue his people. And again, the way to freedom is to trust in the sacrifice God provides.

But this time, God hasn't just *provided* the sacrifice. In Jesus, God has come to *be* the sacrifice—to die instead of his people, so they can be set free.

What's one way in which you could regularly remind yourself of everything God has done for you?

PRAYER

Lord Jesus, thank you for coming to my rescue, even when it meant having your body broken and your blood poured out in my place. Thank you that I can be free from sin. Amen.

⊠ DAY 87 ⊠
ABANDONED ★

READ MARK 14 v 27-31

Have you ever promised you'd be there for someone, and then let them down?

As they head out of the city and back to the Mount of Olives, Jesus drops another bombshell on his disciples: after all these months and months of following him everywhere, tonight they're all going to abandon him. *When the shepherd gets attacked*, God's prophet Zechariah said, *his sheep run in all directions*—and when Jesus gets arrested, the eleven disciples he has left are going to run for it too.

When Peter tries to deny it, Jesus' response is like a bucket of cold water: *You think you're my most loyal friend? Before the sun comes up, you're going to pretend you don't even know me—three times!*

Peter refuses to believe him. Even if *all* the others run, even if staying means *dying*, he swears he'll stick with Jesus to the end.

The other disciples all say the same—and they're all wrong.

Judas has already slipped away to lead the chief priests to Jesus. When they get here, every single one of his disciples is going to freak out and run away.

Jesus isn't just going to die. He's going to die *alone*, abandoned by his closest friends.

It's a dark chapter in their relationship. But Jesus has already provided a glimmer of hope that it won't be the *last* chapter: "After I have risen, I will go ahead of you into Galilee" (v 28). Yes, they're all going to run. But Jesus says they'll have a chance to turn back.

Jesus *knows* this is what his disciples are like. He knows this is what *people* are like. He knows all of us ignore and forget God, and make terrible decisions as a result.

But that's exactly why Jesus came. And having paid for all of our mistakes with his death, Jesus is ready and willing to welcome us back to himself.

Do you feel like you've run far away from Jesus? What if it's not too late to turn back?

PRAYER

Loving God, I'm sorry for when I let you down. Thank you that I can never run so far away that you can't find me and bring me home. Amen.

TORN APART ★

READ MARK 14 v 32-42 ✦

Imagine someone you met yesterday suddenly announces they're walking out of your life. How do you feel?

Probably fine, since you barely know them anyway.

But now think of your oldest, closest relationship—the person you love most in the whole world. Imagine *they* announce that they're leaving you.

That's a completely different story, right? The older and closer the relationship, the more devastating it is to have it torn apart.

Jesus walks through the night, knowing there's a mob coming for him. Suddenly, he's overwhelmed with emotion—he's so miserable that it feels like dying. Asking his disciples to stand guard, Jesus heads alone into the darkness. He collapses to the ground, begging his Father to get him out of what's coming next.

Isn't there *any* other way they can do this?

Obviously, Jesus has seen his death coming. He knows the physical pain will be unbearable. But that's not what's breaking him.

When we sin—when we run from God—we're cutting ourselves off from the source of all life and love. And so the consequence of sin is *losing* our lives and becoming totally *separated* from God's love. *This* is what Jesus means when he talks about hell.

And to truly take our place, *this* is what Jesus will have to experience. Not just physical death. *Total separation from God his Father.* Remember, the older and closer the relationship, the more devastating it is to have it torn apart—and Jesus has an *infinitely close* relationship with God his Father, stretching back *literally forever*.

That's what Jesus is about to lose. And even the first taste of that devastation is enough to bring him down to the ground in agony.

But Jesus knows there's no other way. He'll do whatever his Father wants him to do. He gets up, wakes his friends and turns to face his betrayer.

What does Jesus' willingness to suffer so terribly tell us about his love for us?

PRAYER

Lord Jesus, thank you that you were willing to do what it took to welcome me home to you. Amen.

★ ✦DAY 89✦

THE ARREST ★

★ READ MARK 14 v 43-52

In a quiet garden, in the dark of night, away from the crowds, Judas has found the ideal time and place to hand Jesus over. It's the perfect opportunity to secretly arrest an innocent man.

Israel's leaders have sent an armed mob to capture Jesus.

As if he's just another violent rebel leader.

As if he hasn't spent years proving that that's *not* what his kingdom is like.

As if they haven't had every chance to arrest Jesus publicly, if he'd actually done anything wrong.

Judas steps forward. He kisses Jesus. It's a traditional sign of respect—but tonight, Judas has given it a dark new meaning. In a world long before photos and videos, not everyone in the mob knows Jesus' face—and so Judas gives them a signal: *this is the one. Come and take him.*

As the mob grabs Jesus, a defender leaps forward, slicing an ear off the high priest's servant. We know from Jesus' other biographies that it was *Peter* who drew the sword—and that Jesus immediately reached out and healed the servant.

If Jesus thought violence was the answer, he could've destroyed this whole mob with a wave of his hand. If he'd wanted to escape, he could've broken free in an instant.

Instead, he lets them take him. It's the only way to fulfil what God has promised—the only way to save his people.

And at that moment, just as Jesus predicted, his friends all run for it.

One of them gets grabbed by the garment he's wearing. He shrugs it off and keeps running, fleeing naked into the night. Only hours ago, Jesus' friends all swore they'd never abandon him. But here they are, so desperate to get away that they'll even leave without their clothes if they have to.

Imagine yourself in the garden that night. What would you have done?

PRAYER

Jesus, you showed such commitment to your friends, even as they ran away from you. Please teach me love and courage like that. Thank you for your commitment to me, too. Amen.

☒DAY 90☒
THE TRIAL

READ MARK 14 v 53-65

Have you ever had someone make up rumours and lies about you? Jesus knows how that feels.

The mob drags him into an emergency meeting of the Sanhedrin, Israel's court. It's the middle of the night, a ludicrous time for a trial. But Israel's leaders want Jesus condemned by morning, before the crowds discover what they're up to. Because if Jesus' supporters find out he's on trial, they'll be furious. But if he's already as good as *dead*... Well, then he can't have been the Messiah after all.

Israel's law said you couldn't declare someone guilty of a crime without two witnesses confirming what had happened. The witnesses were separated and asked the same set of questions about the event. If their answers didn't match, their evidence didn't count.

And even though Israel's leaders deliberately organise witnesses to lie about Jesus, they still can't get their stories to agree—which means they have no evidence against him. Eventually, they'll have to let him go. You can sense the high priest's frustration. *Defend yourself! Are you the Messiah or not?*

Jesus has complete control over his situation. He could just stay quiet and watch their whole case fall apart. Instead, he tells them the truth (v 62)—which, even though he's innocent, gives them everything they need to say he's guilty.

Now that Jesus has claimed straight up that he's the Messiah, they can take him to the Romans and say he's a rival king trying to overthrow Caesar.

On top of that, by saying that they'll see him sitting at God's right hand and coming on the clouds of heaven, Jesus is saying that he's equal with God—which (if you're not God) is against Israel's own laws.

Jesus *isn't* trying to overthrow Caesar. He *is* equal with God.

But Israel's leaders don't want the *truth*. They just want an excuse to drag Jesus in front of the Romans—and finally, thanks to Jesus himself, they've got one.

How do you think you would have reacted if you were in Jesus' shoes? What does Jesus' response tell us about him?

PRAYER

God, thank you that, because of his love for me, Jesus didn't shrink back from suffering. Amen.

★ 🎬 DAY 91 🎬

DENYING JESUS

READ MARK 14 v 66-72

Have you ever had a moment when the weight of a bad decision came crashing down on you—when you found yourself drowning in guilt, sure you'd ruined everything, sure there was *nothing* you could do to fix it?

As Peter waits outside for Jesus' trial to finish, it seems like he might actually keep his promise to stick with Jesus to the end—until a servant-girl recognises his face in the firelight.

I've seen you with Jesus!

Peter's courage evaporates. He tells her she's wrong and heads for the door. But the servant-girl follows, pointing him out again.

He's one of them!

Again, Peter denies it. But as others turn to look, they're convinced too.

Surely you were with Jesus! You even share his Galilean accent!

Only hours ago, Peter said he'd rather *die* than abandon Jesus. But now, for the third time tonight, he swears he doesn't even know him.

The cockcrow is like a knife in Peter's heart. He breaks down sobbing, sure he's ruined everything, sure there's nothing he can do to fix it. And he's right. There's nothing he can do. But that doesn't mean it can't be fixed.

We know from Jesus' other biographies that Peter's story doesn't end here. After rising from the dead, Jesus came to find Peter, and he forgave him (John 21 v 15-19). Their friendship was restored, and Peter spent the rest of his life spreading the good news of the kingdom that he'd been welcomed back into.

This is exactly why Jesus came: because we've *all* made a mess of our relationship with God that we can't fix. But Jesus has come to take our place and put those broken friendships back together. If you turn back to him, there's nothing in the world he won't forgive.

Do you feel like you've messed up too badly for God to still love you? What would Jesus say to that?

PRAYER

Loving God, when I mess up, please help me to be quick to return to you, knowing you're always ready to forgive me. Amen.

☒ DAY 92 ☒
PILATE

★ READ MARK 15 V 1-5

Israel's leaders have decided that Jesus deserves death. Unfortunately for them, they don't actually have the authority to kill him.

Only the Romans are allowed to put criminals to death, so the mob drags Jesus, bruised and bleeding, to Pilate, the Roman ruler in charge of Jerusalem and Judea.

Israel's leaders know Pilate won't care if Jesus is a false teacher or if he's pretending to be equal with their God. These things might *infuriate* the Sanhedrin, but they won't concern Pilate at all. Instead, the chief priests twist Jesus' words into something that will get Pilate's attention: *This man says he's the true king of our people—the king of the Jews! He wants to overthrow Caesar!*

Pilate doesn't care about Israel's God or Israel's law, but he *does* care about keeping Israel's *people* under control. If Jesus *is* a rival king plotting a rebellion, Pilate needs to deal with him.

At the same time, Pilate's no fan of Israel's leaders either. If he can, he wouldn't mind releasing Jesus, just to flex his power over them.

But when Pilate asks if the accusations are true, Jesus refuses to defend himself. Pilate is amazed. Anyone else in Jesus' position would be lying or begging or *something*. But Jesus keeps silent.

Remember, centuries earlier, the prophet Isaiah had promised God's people that a servant would come and suffer for their sins to bring them peace with God (Isaiah 53). Even in the face of death, this servant wouldn't fight or argue. He'd go quietly, like a lamb being led to the slaughter. But then somehow, after his death, the servant would return to life.

Jesus knows *exactly* who he is. He knows he's exactly where he needs to be.

He's not here to fight or argue. He's here to suffer. But through that suffering, he's here to win.

How do you think Jesus stayed so determined, even in the face of such awful suffering?

PRAYER

Loving God, thank you that Jesus was willing to suffer in order to beat death for us. Please teach me to trust you like Jesus did, especially when life feels hard and unfair. Amen.

✄ DAY 93 ✄
BARABBAS
READ MARK 15 v 6-15

For Pilate, keeping the people of Israel under control is a tricky balancing act. If he doesn't treat them harshly, they won't obey him—but if he treats them *too* harshly, they might get fed up and rebel against him.

Part of the solution is customs like this: each year at Passover, when the people are most on edge about Roman rule, Pilate releases a prisoner of their choice as a way of saying, *See how reasonable I can be?*

This year, Pilate offers them Jesus—but the chief priests snap into action, moving through the crowd:

Not Jesus! Barabbas! Give us Barabbas!

Barabbas is a murderer—a violent, Rome-hating rebel. He's exactly the kind of man Israel's leaders have just accused Jesus of being! But the chief priests stir the crowd up to ask for Barabbas instead.

What about your king? Pilate asks. *What should I do with him?*

Nail him to a cross! Crucify him!

Pilate can see things are getting out of hand. If he doesn't do something soon, he'll be dealing with a full-blown riot.

He has a choice: he can do what's he knows is right or do what's best for himself.

Pilate makes his choice.

He gives the order, releasing a murderer to the crowd and sending a man he knows is innocent to be flogged and killed.

Have you ever followed the crowd into making a terrible decision? How did the situation turn out?

PRAYER

Dear God, it's so easy to do what's best for me instead of doing what's right, especially when it means I get to follow along with the crowd. Please give me the wisdom and courage I need to live the way *you* call me to live. Amen.

⛏DAY 94⛏

HAIL TO THE KING!

READ MARK 15 v 15-20

By the time Jesus leaves Pilate, he's already half-dead—because before Pilate sends him to be crucified, he first has Jesus flogged.

Jesus is tied down, while soldiers take turns beating him with a whip made from leather cords with pieces of jagged metal or bone woven through them.

It wasn't unusual for prisoners to die from these floggings—but Jesus survives.

The soldiers take him into the palace. The idea that this pathetic wreck of a man could ever think he was king is an absolute joke to them—one they decide to have some fun with before he dies.

They dress Jesus up, draping a royal robe over his shoulders and twisting thorns into a crown to jam onto his head.

Look everyone! Here he is! Come and see the mighty king of Israel!

They bludgeon his head with a staff, over and over again.

They spit on his trembling body.

They drop to their knees, bowing down in fake adoration.

We praise you, your Majesty! Hail to the king!

It's unbearably cruel. But it's also a picture of how people have treated God since the beginning—denying that he's the king and rejecting his authority over us.

At the same time, it's a picture of Jesus' response to sin. He could destroy his enemies in a second, but he doesn't. He doesn't fight back or run away.

He takes the worst hatred and mockery and rejection that humanity can throw at him—and then he heads to the cross, to pay back our betrayal with love.

Is there anyone you know who thinks that Jesus is a joke? What do you think Jesus would want you to say to them?

PRAYER

Lord Jesus, sorry for the times I've ignored or rejected you. Thank you that, instead of paying back evil for evil, you overcame evil with good. Please teach me to do the same. Amen.

THE CROSS ★

READ MARK 15 v 21-32

★

Jesus is led back outside the city, to "the place of the skull", to suffer a death so horrible that no citizen of Rome is ever allowed to go through it.

Crucifixion is a punishment reserved just for the nations the empire has conquered. It's designed to torture Rome's enemies to death as slowly, painfully and humiliatingly as possible—out in public, where everyone can see. Because it's not just a punishment. It's a warning to anyone watching: *Mess with Rome, and we'll do this to you next.*

Taking Jesus' clothes to keep for themselves, the soldiers hold him down against the cross, stretching him out naked on his back. They hammer a nail through each of his wrists and a third one through his ankles, pinning him to the wood.

The soldiers lift up the cross and plant it in the ground. Jesus hangs in the air, the full weight of his body dragging down on those three nails.

As Jesus writhes in pain, his enemies come forward to laugh at his suffering.

"He saved others ... but he can't save himself!" (v 31).

(But, as Jesus has been telling his disciples for months, refusing to save himself is exactly *how* he's going to save others.)

"Come down now from the cross, that we may see and believe" (v 32).

(But if they didn't believe the other miracles, why would they believe this one?)

Of course, Jesus could come down anytime he wanted. It's strength, not weakness, keeping him there.

Moment by moment, Jesus *chooses* to stay nailed to the cross. He chooses the path of pain and suffering, mockery and humiliation, all to save and forgive God's lost children—even the ones hurling abuse at him.

Author Sally Lloyd-Jones puts it perfectly: "It wasn't the nails that kept Jesus there. It was love."

What does it say about Jesus, that he was willing to suffer a death like this? What does it say about us, that he had to?

PRAYER

Jesus, thank you for staying committed to me, even at my worst, so that I can be forgiven. Please help me to show the same love and commitment to others. Amen.

⬛ DAY 96 ⬛

FORSAKEN ★

★
★ READ MARK 15 v 33-36 ★

For three long hours, Jesus hangs on the cross, as the morning sun climbs across the sky.

Then suddenly, the sun *stops* climbing.

It stops shining altogether. Day turns to night.

And in the darkness, Jesus cries out, "My God, my God, why have you forsaken me?" (v 34).

Wait. What?

Why does Jesus suddenly sound like he doesn't know what's going on? Has he failed somehow? Has something gone wrong?

The truth is, Jesus knows *exactly* what he's doing.

His words aren't *just* a cry of despair. They're a quote— the opening line of a song written by Jesus' ancestor, King David.

The song, Psalm 22, describes a man surrounded by enemies who insult and mock him. His clothes are taken away and divided among his enemies. The man's enemies pierce his hands and feet. They lay him in the dust of death.

But the song doesn't stop there. By the end of the song, the forsaken one is alive and well and no longer abandoned by God.

And so, yes, Jesus cries out because he really *is* being forsaken by God his Father—because he's taking the punishment that our sins deserve. And Jesus really *is* completely overwhelmed with horror and misery at what's happening to him.

But by crying out with *these* words, Jesus shows that he also knows where this story ends: not in death but in victory. And so he chooses to *keep* trusting in God his Father, even as God turns his back on him.

Jesus obeys God to the end and gets forsaken, so that we, who *haven't* obeyed God, will never have to learn what being forsaken by God feels like.

Do you ever feel abandoned by God? How can Jesus' death reassure you that you aren't?

PRAYER

Lord Jesus, thank you that you were forsaken by God so I could be forgiven. When I feel abandoned, remind me that you're *always* with me and always will be. Amen.

★ ◤DAY 97◥

THE CURTAIN

★ READ MARK 15 v 37-41 ★

Deep inside the temple—past the courts where the people came to pray and worship, past the altar where the priests made their sacrifices—was the Most Holy Place: the place where God's presence came to dwell among his people.

The Most Holy Place was blocked off from the rest of the temple by a heavy curtain. The curtain was a barrier, separating the people from the presence of God. It was a symbol of the *true* barrier between people and God caused by our sin.

Only the high priest was allowed to pass through the curtain to the Most Holy Place, and only once a year, and only after he'd made a sacrifice—an animal had to die for the sins of the people.

For centuries the curtain sent a clear message to God's people: *Because of your sin, you can't be close to God.*

But then, on the cross, Jesus cries out with his dying breath...

And the curtain is torn in two.

Not from the bottom, where a person could reach, but from the *top*.

As Jesus dies, God himself rips the barrier to the Most Holy Place *wide open*.

Why? Because through the death of Jesus, the sin that separates us from God has finally been paid for, once and for all. Jesus' death is the sacrifice that all the other sacrifices have been pointing to—the sacrifice to *end* all sacrifices.

Which means that, no matter who you are or what you might have done to separate yourself from God and his kingdom, all you need to do is put your trust in what Jesus has done for you on the cross, and you can be welcomed back home to God again.

This is the good news that Mark has been wanting to tell us all along.

How will you respond to it?

PRAYER

Lord Jesus, thank you for doing everything it took to tear down the barrier between me and God. Please keep showing me more and more clearly why this is such good news for me. Amen.

✖ DAY 98 ✖
THE TOMB ★

READ MARK 15 v 42-47 ✦

Joseph of Arimathea is an important member of the Sanhedrin, which means he was at the chief priest's house for Jesus' trial. But surprisingly, Joseph is also a follower of Jesus, waiting for God's kingdom.

At least, he *was*. Joseph probably thinks those hopes have died along with Jesus. Still, he at least wants to give Jesus a proper burial. But he'll have to move fast.

It's already late Friday afternoon. The Sabbath begins at sunset. If he doesn't bury Jesus by then, it'll have to wait until Sunday morning, because burying someone counts as work (and the Sabbath is a day of rest). In the meantime, Jesus' body might be left hanging in the open for birds to attack, or else dumped somewhere by the Romans.

It's a gutsy move, asking Pilate for Jesus' body. If the Sanhedrin hear what Joseph's up to, they'll be furious. And there's always the chance that Pilate himself might decide to take out his frustration at Israel's leaders on Joseph.

Fortunately, it turns out that Pilate doesn't care *what* happens to Jesus' body. But he does want to make sure Jesus really is dead.

And we should want to make sure too—because if Jesus *actually* died and came back to life, that changes everything.

But if he never really died, if he just got badly hurt and then recovered...

Well, that's not so miraculous after all.

Thankfully, Mark gives us the details: Pilate checks with the centurion and learns that, yes, Jesus really is dead (and as a professional killer, the centurion has *zero* chance of getting this wrong).

Joseph retrieves Jesus' body. He buries it in a tomb, sealed with a massive stone. And from Jesus' other biographies, we know that Pilate even sends armed soldiers to stand guard outside, just in case anyone tries to steal the body.

By nightfall, Jesus is dead and buried. It's over.

Well, for a couple of days, anyway.

Why do you think Mark thought it was important to describe Jesus' death and burial in such detail?

PRAYER

Dear God, thank you for this incredible true story—and thank you that it doesn't end here. Amen.

RESURRECTION

READ MARK 16 v 1-8

All through Saturday, it looks like Jesus has been defeated.

Defeated by the Sanhedrin. Defeated by the Romans. Defeated by death itself.

So when these friends of Jesus visit his tomb on Sunday morning, they're not checking if he's alive. They *know* there's no hope of that. They just want to finish the burial that got so rushed through on Friday.

But as they arrive, they realise someone else has got here first. The tomb is wide open.

Who did this? Has some cruel enemy of Jesus come and stolen his body?

The women peer inside. Sure enough, Jesus' body is missing. But the tomb's not empty.

A man sits inside—just calmly hanging out in the tomb,

like he's waiting for them. He's an angel, a messenger from heaven. His message will change the world forever:

Jesus is alive!

Through his resurrection, Jesus proves he's *exactly* who he says he is—the Messiah, the Son of God. It's what Mark has been saying right from the first sentence of his book.

Jesus is the King who will rule God's kingdom forever. One day, when Jesus returns, he'll bring that kingdom with him to redeem and restore the whole world. The hungry will be fed. The slaves will be freed. The sick will be healed. The dead will be raised to life.

And every single person who has put their faith in what Jesus has done for them on the cross will be welcomed into God's kingdom with open arms—welcomed into perfect, never-ending life with God. Just as Jesus was raised to new life, we'll be raised to new life too.

But in the meantime, Jesus invites everyone, everywhere, to follow him and to start living the abundant kingdom-of-God lives we were made for, right here, right now.

What do you think this means for us here and now, today?

PRAYER

Lord Jesus, thank you for your resurrection, which proves that your rescue plan worked! Please show me how to live as a citizen of your kingdom here and now, while I wait for you to bring that kingdom in all its fullness. Amen.

⚡ DAY 100 ⚡

THE EXTRA ENDING

READ MARK 16 v 9-20

Back before printers and copiers, the only way to share a book you'd written was to carefully copy the whole thing out by hand. And so, as the good news of Jesus exploded through the ancient world, that's exactly what people did with Mark's Gospel—over and over and over again.

One of the reasons we can be certain that the Bible we have today hasn't been changed over time is that the many ancient copies we still have all match up with each other.

There's just one section in Mark's Gospel that doesn't quite fit.

As you began today's reading, you hopefully found a note in your Bible telling you that these last twelve verses don't actually appear in the earliest copies of Mark's Gospel.

So why are they here?

Well, when you think about it, Mark's *actual* ending, which we explored yesterday, is pretty strange and sudden.

The women find out Jesus is alive.

They run trembling from the tomb, and...

The End.

Weird, right? In fact, the ending is so abrupt that centuries later, some unknown writer apparently decided to "fix" it by adding an ending of their own. They took bits of Jesus' other three biographies in the Bible, mixed them together, and made this.

So, actually, most of the information here is absolutely true.

We know the resurrected Jesus appeared first to Mary Magdalene, then to two others walking along the road, and then to the eleven disciples (Luke 24 v 1-35).

We know Jesus gave them convincing proof that he really *was* alive again (John 20 v 19-29). We know he sent his followers out to share the good news with the whole world (Matthew 28 v 16-20). And we know he returned to heaven, the triumphant King of the whole universe (Acts 1 v 1-11).

But even though all that stuff is *true*, it still doesn't belong in *Mark's* Gospel.

Which brings us back to *why* Mark's original ending is so abrupt.

Some experts think Mark originally wrote a bit more of an ending, but then it got lost. Others think Mark's sudden ending is deliberate—that as we wonder about Jesus' friends' responses to his resurrection, it's meant to get us thinking about our *own* response to Jesus.

Either way, as we reach the end of Mark's Gospel, we're left with one all-important question:

Now that Jesus has risen from the dead, proving that he really is the Messiah, the Son of God... what are you going to do about it?

PRAYER

Loving God, thank you for the good news of Jesus, recorded so faithfully in Mark's Gospel. Please take what I've seen and heard, and use it to transform my whole life. Amen.

References

The reason I was able to write this book is not because I am some kind of Bible genius. It's because, in God's kindness, my life has been filled with countless men and women who have helped me understand what Jesus shows us about himself through the Bible. If I tried to name every one of them, this book would be twice as thick—but there are a few people in particular whose work deserves special mention:

Back in 2007, I listened (via podcast) to a sermon series called *The Story of the Christ*, preached by Jeff Manion at Ada Bible Church. These sermons had a huge impact on my understanding of the life of Jesus, and I'm sure they've shaped this book in ways I don't even realise. In particular, the "u-turn" idea on Day 6 is borrowed straight from one of those teachings.

In 2013, I travelled through Israel on a study tour led by John Dickson, Simon Smart and Stephen Langfur, who opened my eyes in a whole new way to the historical background to Mark's Gospel. This would be a much different (and worse) book without them.

Timothy Keller's book, *King's Cross*, along with the sermon series upon which it's based, were immensely helpful to me in the writing of this book. Days 9, 13, 19, 33, 34, 50, 51, 61 and 72 of *Best News Ever* all include bits of wisdom I picked up from Keller.

The Jesus Storybook Bible by Sally Lloyd-Jones is the most beautifully written Bible storybook I have ever read. I've quoted it at the end of Day 95, but you really should go and read the whole thing.

The videos by Tim Mackie, Jon Collins, and the team at The Bible Project were a valuable resource, as well as The Bible Project Podcast, and Tim Mackie's teaching podcast, Exploring My Strange Bible. In particular, my explanations of Mark 13 owe a huge debt to Tim Mackie's teaching on the parallel verses in Matthew 24.

◣ Thank yous ◢

Thanks to Carl Laferton for taking a chance on a Bible-reading book by a guy who'd only ever written sci-fi novels—and to Rachel Jones and the whole team at TGBC for your incredible help and support in bringing this thing into the world.

Huge thanks to Ella Figliuzzi and Rebekah Norman, who read *Best News Ever* first. Your enthusiasm for this book has been so encouraging! Thanks also to Elisa Chamoun, Chris Coffee, Stuart Coulton, Micah Ford, Tom French, Corlette Graham, Davo Gunning, Philip Kern and Madison Soh for your advice and feedback on different bits and pieces along the way.

Thanks to my parents, Cass and Peter, for introducing me to the good news and showing me how to live it out. Thanks to Katie and Waz, Phil and Meredith, Kerryn and Andrew, and James and Hanri for all the support, encouragement and laughs. Pack your bags: we're going to Grappa!

Thanks to Phil and Georgie Kern for believing in this thing from the beginning (and pre-ordering it seven months early).

Thanks to Rowan McAuley for all the chats about God and life and writing. Let's write another book together soon!

Thanks to my church family, past and present, at Abbotsford Presbyterian. Thanks also to everyone who's ever come along to KCentral or YCentral—I hope you love this book, and I hope it helps you see even more clearly how awesome Jesus is!

Thanks to my awesome chaplaincy colleagues, Cathy, Eddy and Jiye. I am so grateful for your friendship and partnership in the gospel (and also for the occasional Nerf-gun skirmishes in the staff room).

More from
Chris Morphew

Big Questions is a series fun and fast-paced books walking young people aged 9-13 through what the Bible says about some of the big questions of life, helping you to grow in confident and considered faith.

thegoodbook.co.uk/big-questions
thegoodbook.com/big-questions

CONTINUE TO
DISCOVER

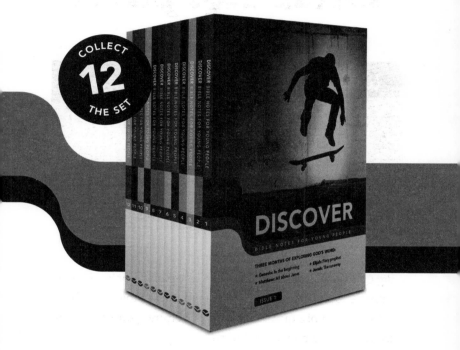

DISCOVER: BIBLE NOTES FOR YOUNG PEOPLE

If you want help to keep reading and understanding the Bible—look no further. *Discover* takes you through the Bible in action-packed, hard-hitting daily chunks. It delivers God's truth straight to you in a no-nonsense way—and it's fun!

With puzzles, prayer and pondering sections: Bible reading has never been so gripping.

thegoodbook.com | thegoodbook.co.uk
thegoodbook.com.au | thegoodbook.co.nz

thegoodbook
COMPANY

BIBLICAL | RELEVANT | ACCESSIBLE

At The Good Book Company, we are dedicated to helping Christians and local churches grow. We believe that God's growth process always starts with hearing clearly what he has said to us through his timeless word—the Bible.

Ever since we opened our doors in 1991, we have been striving to produce Bible-based resources that bring glory to God. We have grown to become an international provider of user-friendly resources to the Christian community, with believers of all backgrounds and denominations using our books, Bible studies, devotionals, evangelistic resources, and DVD-based courses.

We want to equip ordinary Christians to live for Christ day by day, and churches to grow in their knowledge of God, their love for one another, and the effectiveness of their outreach.

Call us for a discussion of your needs or visit one of our local websites for more information on the resources and services we provide.

Your friends at The Good Book Company

thegoodbook.com | thegoodbook.co.uk
thegoodbook.com.au | thegoodbook.co.nz
thegoodbook.co.in